We are on the verge of a great harvest. The Lord wants to bring a paradigm shift to the Body of Christ and dismantle old religious wineskins of evangelism with new Spirit-breathed strategies. Doug Addison's book, *Prophecy, Dreams, and Evangelism* is one of God's change agents. Birthed from Doug's own journey out of darkness into the light, this book trumpets a call for the Church to move relationally among the lost and see them through the eyes and heart of Jesus. This is an insightful evangelism handbook for all believers.

—JILL AUSTIN
President of Master Potter Ministries, Hollywood, CA

Prophesy, Dreams, and Evangelism is a first fruits answer for our generation who want to effectively share their love for Jesus but don't know where to start. Doug Addison brings evangelism back to the simple practice of valuing those we would meet and love. He is both vulnerable in his testimony and practical in his teaching, and he gives us an inspiring book.

—SHAWN BOLZ
Author, *The Throne Room Company*

Every lover of God should read *Prophecy, Dreams and Evangelism: Revealing God's Love Through Divine Encounters*. Doug Addison develops a revolutionary approach to demonstrate God's saving, delivering love. He highlights the tools God is currently breathing on to inspire believers to touch the dark world with hope and the Creator's spiritual light.

—BARBIE L. BREATHITT
Breath of the Spirit Ministries

When I think of the term "a man after God's own heart" Doug Addison is one who comes to mind. His passion for God and the lost is contagious. I have personally witnessed the effectiveness of prophetic outreaches that Doug leads. God's hand is on this man and this method. Read and absorb the insights contained in this timely book.

—AARON EVANS
Founder, BridgeBuilders International

I can't imagine a more practical book on evangelism. Neither can I imagine a more supernatural book on evangelism. *Prophecy, Dreams, and Evangelism* is the most profound book I've seen on the subject. It is both timely and necessary. This you can try at home!

—BILL JOHNSON
Author and Senior Pastor, Bethel Church, Redding, CA

Prophecy, Dreams, and Evangelism is a great book. Read it—and then go!
—PATRICIA KING
Founder, Extreme Prophetic

Prophecy, Dreams, and Evangelism is a wake-up call for the Church. Doug Addison's unique style and cutting-edge approach to ministry makes him one of the leading voices of prophetic evangelism today. I highly recommend both Doug's ministry and this valuable book. The grace and wisdom revealed in these pages will revolutionize your understanding of Jesus' commission to touch the world with the message of God's love.
—LARRY RANDOLPH
Larry Randolph Ministries, Redding, CA

After reading Doug Addison's book *Prophecy, Dreams, and Evangelism* you will not be intimidated by the "E-word" (Evangelism) any longer. You will be spurred on to discover creative ways to have more divine encounters!
—RECIE SAUNDERS
National Ministry Team Coordinator, Streams Ministries International

I have always thought that the prophetic and evangelism were integrally connected. This book excites me. It says much of what I have thought over the years but didn't have the time or energy or creativity to pen myself! Doug Addison has done the Church a great service in the writing of this new book. It's a great addition to my library of books on evangelism. Personally, I think this is one of the best books on evangelism to come out in the past few years.
—STEVE SJOGREN
Author of *Irresistible Evangelism, 101 Ways to Reach Your Community, Conspiracy of Kindness, Seeing Beyond Church Walls,* and other books.

PROPHECY, DREAMS, and EVANGELISM

Revealing God's
Love Through
Divine Encounters

DOUG ADDISON

STREAMS PUBLISHING HOUSE

Managing Editor and Creative Director: Carolyn Blunk
Contributing Editor: Ernie Freeman
Revision Editor: Dorian Kreindler
Assistant Editor: Mary Ballotte
Editorial Assistant: Leslie Herrier
Designed by: Mike Bailey Design

ISBN: 1-58483-1030

Library of Congress Control Number: 2005926300

Printed in the United States of America.

Dedicated to my loving wife, Linda.

"A wife of noble character who can find?
She is worth far more than rubies."
—Proverbs 31:10

ACKNOWLEDGMENTS

I am grateful to God who brought me out of extreme darkness and into His extreme light so I could take this journey and find new ways of reaching people with His love. I am also grateful for my wife Linda, who has joined me in this journey and has tolerated my hectic travel schedule. And to my daughter Amanda who helps me understand God's love and grace. Also to my sisters Debra and Glenna who prayed for me over the years. Thank you, Ray Etter for becoming my father when I did not have one.

Thanks to John Paul Jackson for teaching me the importance of character and all the positive ways he influenced my life and accelerated my launch into the ministry. A big thank you to Greg and Patty Mapes and all the staff at Streams Ministries, who are more than colleagues, they are family. I would like to acknowledge Carolyn Blunk for encouraging me to write and the great job she did art directing and editing my book.

I owe much to Robert Navarra, Pastors Ben and Christy Pierce, Sharon Waldorf, Brett Johnson, my friends at First Presbyterian Church of San Mateo, Calif., and Pastor Charlie Brown who encouraged me early on to pursue God's destiny for my life.

I am grateful for Phil Zaldatte and Steve Maddox, who laid the foundation for much of the dream team evangelism being done today. And I'd like to thank the many, many people who have traveled with me and helped lead outreaches that provided research required to complete this book. I also want to offer my heartfelt gratitude to Phyllis Watson and Jeannine Rodriguez who spent hours editing and gaining permissions as well as the many others who helped in small but important ways.

CONTENTS

FOREWORD

A round the world, God is using prophetic evangelism, especially biblical dream interpretation, to draw people to Himself.

An offshoot of "power evangelism," a phrase coined by John Wimber in the 1980s, prophetic evangelism uses words of knowledge, prophetic insight, and biblical dream interpretation to lead people to Jesus.

God still does amazing things today that He did in biblical times. In fact, God is pouring out His Spirit in greater measure and accelerating the use of dreams to communicate with all of humanity.

> "And it shall come to pass afterward
> That I will pour out My Spirit on all flesh;
> Your sons and daughters shall prophesy,
> Your old men shall dream dreams,
> Your young men shall see visions.
> And also on My menservants and on My maidservants
> I will pour out My Spirit in those days."
> —Joel 2:28–29 (also referenced in Acts 2:16–21)

When we read Joel's prophesy, we find that the result of prophetic utterances, dreams, visions, and signs and wonders is to bring a harvest into God's Kingdom. Biblical dream interpretation can be used as a tool for helping people come to know and understand God's love for them.

God is giving unsaved people dreams, often warning them not to go down a certain dark path. Instead of turning to God, however, they look elsewhere for the interpretation.

Prophetic evangelism teams are discovering that often after hearing a dream's true interpretation, people are giving their lives to the Lord. When team members share prophetic impressions that God gives them, the prophetic Spirit of God begins to unlock peoples' hearts. Tears begin rolling down peoples' faces as they realize God has been speaking to them all along. Through biblical dream interpretation, people are being touched by God in profound ways.

In late 2001, Doug Addison began working for me as the Streams National Dream Team Coordinator. In February 2002 I sent him to Salt Lake City, Utah to lead a prophetic evangelism outreach at the Winter Olympics. Over five days, Doug and the team interpreted more than one hundred and fifty dreams. One night inside a Starbucks coffee house, two team members were chatting about dreams. As they glanced over at the lineup of thirty shivering people, they offered to interpret anyone's dream. A journalist from Reuters news agency was the first to sit down and share a dream. When our team gave her the interpretation, she looked astonished and fell back in her chair. Before she was finished, a throng of people lined up behind her.

Then in May 2002, I sent Doug to Orlando, Florida to lead a prophetic evangelism workshop with Phil Zaldatte, a former Streams intern who is now in full-time ministry. After teaching about prophetic evangelism, they led an outreach at a nearby shopping mall. One team, upon seeing a woman with a withered hand and a limp, approached her and began to pray for her. Suddenly the woman's withered hand opened and her feet straightened! She was so excited that she invited Jesus into her heart. Another team interpreted a woman's dream. She was so touched that she gave her heart to Jesus in the mall's food court and in front of her friends. That afternoon, fourteen people came to know Jesus and several were healed.

Real life experiences like these have led me to conclude that prophetic evangelism—a reliance on listening to God while sharing the Gospel—is an innovative strategy to grow the Church and introduce Jesus to your unsaved friends.

Prophetic evangelism, especially dream interpretation, is a model God developed in the Bible. The prophet Daniel sought God's wisdom in interpreting dreams, solving riddles, and explaining spiritual mysteries. In fact, Scripture says that among all the astrologers, seers, psychics, and magicians in Babylon, none had more spiritual insight than Daniel (Daniel 1:17–21).

As a young man, Daniel prophesied to King Nebuchadnezzar about a dream the king had. The impact of Daniel's interpretation was so powerful the king exclaimed, "Truly your God is the God of gods, the Lord of kings, and a revealer of secrets, since you could reveal this secret," (Daniel

2:47). Years later, Daniel interpreted another dream for Nebuchadnezzar. After that dream and its interpretation had come to pass, the king again worshipped God (Daniel 4:37). True dreams from God generate a divine curiosity, a question that we're desperate to answer. Unsaved kings like Joseph's Pharoah and Daniel's Nebuchadnezzar scoured the nations for an interpretation to their dreams.

Scripture tells us that dreams are a means of divine communication:

> For God may speak in one way, or in another, yet man does not perceive it. In a dream, in a vision of the night, when deep sleep falls upon men, while slumbering on their beds, then He opens the ears of men, and seals their instruction.
> —Job 33:14–16, NKJV

Forever mindful of us, God faithfully guides us both day and night, as He never sleeps (Psalm 121:3–4). When we sleep, God has our undivided attention, and thus can impart messages into our spirits and seal their instructions.

Every night, God whispers into the dreams of unsaved men and women. He seals the truth within their heart. Prophetic evangelism provides a human voice to the spiritual mysteries God has implanted in the lost. Many will search the world over, looking for the key to unlock that truth. They search the New Age movement, thinking the answer might be there. They go to psychics, astrologers, and tarot card readers looking for the key. They seek out secular dream interpreters who offer Freudian, Jungian, or Gestalt dream analysis. What is most remarkable, Christians, who hear and understand God's voice, hold the key for these wanderers.

For one reason or another, many people outside the Church have had difficulty connecting with God. Prophetic evangelism is just one way to help nudge people closer to a deeper understanding of God's love for them. As spiritual interpretations are applied to dreams, unsaved people are often bewildered to learn that God has been speaking to them all along.

This is the hour for prophetic evangelism—for God's light to shine on people who have waited years for a resolution in their lives. This is a moment in history where Christians can make a massive difference—

one person and one dream at a time.

We are standing on the threshold of a new spiritual awakening. God is getting ready to unleash a powerful wave of prophetic evangelism, larger than any of us has ever dreamed. And with it will come a harvest that is unprecedented in Church history. It's my prayer that this wonderful book by Doug Addison will help facilitate this harvest.

—John Paul Jackson
Founder, Streams Ministries International

INTRODUCTION

I t is hard not to notice a new spiritual hunger in people today. On television talk shows people are discussing spiritual things; psychics and tarot card readers who once operated in dark tents at carnivals now occupy plush offices and kiosks in shopping malls. It's not unusual for a high school student to be part of a Wiccan coven or to be found in the occult section of a bookstore looking up spells and incantations in one of the many New Age books lining the shelves.

With this increasing interest in the spiritual realm and the occult, one cannot help but wonder why this is happening. Did dark spiritual forces suddenly invade the minds of people? Or has God Himself planted a spiritual hunger that incites people to search for understanding and spiritual fulfillment? I believe it is the latter.

On the day of Pentecost, Peter rose up and recited a portion of a prophecy from the Old Testament book of Joel: "In the last days, God says, I will pour out my Spirit on all people" (Acts 2:17a). Many assume God is speaking about the Church, but this Scripture does not say He will pour out His Spirit only on Christians but on everyone. This is apparent in verse 18: "Even on my servants, both men and women, I will pour out my Spirit in those days…" God says He will pour out His Spirit on everyone, including His followers. The result of this lavish outpouring is that suddenly men and women will become aware of their emptiness and need for purpose, direction, and truth in life. God will use various circumstances and events to draw people to Himself.

Many followers of Jesus have been crying out to God for revival. A wave of revival swept the world in the late 1960s when disillusioned hippies and young people, who had been searching fruitlessly for love, peace, and tranquility, suddenly began to turn to Jesus. These stinky, long-haired Jesus people began showing up at churches, but the churches were not quite ready for a revival lacking shoes or deodorant!

Out of that move of God's Spirit sprang up new churches such as the Calvary Chapels and the Vineyard Christian Fellowships. John Wimber, the founder of the Vineyard movement and former member of the Righteous Brothers band, wrote a book called *Power Evangelism* describing a new sort of evangelism. *Power Evangelism* was a call for Christians to step out and trust God to reveal to them the people He is drawing. Believers were then encouraged to ask God for spiritual gifts needed to help lead these "seekers" to Jesus, such as praying for their healing or encouraging them with a prophetic word to spur them on.

Many considered this method of reaching people with God's love radical and even controversial but could not dispute its effectiveness. However, any cutting-edge move of God if not kept alive and practiced on a regular basis will lose its sharpness and like *Power Evangelism* will be largely forgotten.

So we continue to cry out for revival, and we continue to devise ways to bring people into God's Kingdom. We may feel like the fishermen in Luke 5 who were tired after fishing all night and catching nothing. Jesus called out and told them to go into deep water and let down their nets once again. Only this time, to their surprise, they caught more fish than they could handle. Similarly, God is calling us to plunge into deep water if we want to catch fish.

God is indeed pouring out His Spirit on all people. As Christians we need only ask Him to point out those He is drawing to Himself. If we ask God to open our eyes to "see" and our ears to "hear" His voice, we can get ready for a number of supernatural and divine encounters specifically designed by God to draw millions to Jesus Christ. I believe a new wave of power and prophetic evangelism is beginning to sweep the world as God calls us to partner with Him in what will be one of the largest revivals in Church history.

Most people are open to talking about spiritual things; they genuinely desire to encounter God's power and they truly seek a spiritual experience. Unfortunately many think Christianity simply means going to church and listening to dry sermons, since they may have tried going to church sometime or went as children, but were not able to connect with God in the church. Some have given up spirituality all together, and others have turned to alternative spiritual avenues such as the New Age or the occult.

If we could step outside the box of our own ideas about how to share God's love, and begin to meet people where they are, perhaps we could also learn to convey biblical truths and be understood by someone unschooled in religion. Maybe then we could perceive the Holy

Spirit showing us how our heavenly Father views people; or that He wants them to know He is aware of a particular pain or struggle in their life. If we offer to interpret a dream for them, and through that they realize God has been speaking to them all along, then it's likely they will let down their walls and suddenly be very open to talking about God.

Prophetic evangelism employs such revelatory gifts as word of knowledge, word of wisdom, prophecy, and dream interpretation to reach people for Jesus Christ. God never intended for these and other gifts like healing or the working of miracles to be relegated to the four walls of the Church, as they have been until recently. The New Testament shows us how Jesus, His disciples, and the apostle Paul all used these gifts from God to reach people. The classic example is in John 4, where Jesus met the Samaritan woman at the well. Jesus "read" her past, present, and even offered her a glimpse of the future. As a result, she evangelized many people in her city for Christ that day.

Luke 5, as mentioned previously, shows Jesus at the shore teaching the people from Simon Peter's boat. Peter and his fishing partners meanwhile were standing on the shore listening to Jesus and mending their nets. Jesus instructed them to put their boat out into deep water and let down their nets for a catch. Peter objected at first because they had been fishing all night and had caught nothing, but because Jesus told them to, he agreed. When they let down their nets, they caught so many fish that the nets began to break. They had to call the other boat for help, and both boats were so full that they nearly sank.

Luke 5 is a great example of the Church in our day. We have been fishing all night and have not caught much. Many of us have not ventured out of the shallow water, out of the zones of safety and comfortableness, to find the fish where they are. The fish are in the deep water; they are outside the Church, and outside our opinions and prejudices. As we are obedient to God's call and venture into the deep water and into relationships with people "on the streets," we will be overwhelmed by the response and will need to network with other churches to accommodate the great numbers of people who will come to Jesus.

Prophetic evangelism could very well be the "deep water" mentioned in Luke 5. Jesus is calling us to let our nets down for a catch so incredible that our boats will be sorely tested! Are you ready?

A Journey
in Sharing
God's Love

CHAPTER
1

MY JOURNEY
to JESUS

At age nineteen I was in such deep spiritual darkness that it took two radical encounters with Jesus to bring me into the Christian life. I had always known about God, and I loved the stories of how Jesus would cast out demons, heal the sick, and raise the dead. I told myself, *If I could see that kind of power, I would believe and give my life to God.*

I had tried going to church several times in my life, but I was very disappointed that the churchgoers believed God no longer chose to do miraculous things today since we now had the Bible and modern medicine. They told me I simply needed to attend services every week, read my Bible every day, pray, and refrain from drinking, smoking, and cussing, and all my problems would be solved. But that somehow never cut it for me because I had been having dark spiritual experiences ever since I was a child. I needed God's power to deliver me from the things that were haunting and tormenting me when I was alone.

I also could not fathom why Christians didn't recognize that God sends us messages. I had been hearing and knowing spiritual things as early as I could remember, although the source was not God. The Christians around me believed that hearing spiritual messages was of the devil, yet the Bible detailed Jesus and His disciples as having these sorts of experiences. This confused me because it seemed to give the devil more power than God. So, though I loved Jesus, church did not satisfy my spiritual hunger, and I eventually became increasingly drawn to the occult and paranormal. Ultimately darkness became my companion.

I had prayed to receive Jesus Christ into my life when I was twelve years old, but my life never changed then. It wasn't until I was nineteen years old that my first real spiritual awakening to Jesus took place. Previously I had been having freak accidents, recurring nightmares, and demonic activity at night in my bedroom.

One day I ran into a witch I was acquainted with from high school, and she agreed to try to help me find relief. She lit a candle, and I saw three visions that all came to pass within a week. I asked her how she approached the spiritual realm, and she told me she used numerology, white witchcraft, and read the Bible. (Note: I am not advocating this erroneous approach to spirituality.)

I responded: "You mean you believe in Jesus?"

"Oh, yeah," she replied, "I love Jesus; I just don't like church."

I agreed with that, so I decided to begin reading my Bible. Within a few weeks I had a spiritual breakthrough! I began to pray. The nightmares and the accidents stopped, the spirits stopped harassing me, and I knew it was because of Jesus.

I went to church a few weeks later on a Sunday morning and talked about seeing visions and encountering witches and demons in my room. I must have frightened and shocked those people, and I was having a déjà-vu experience: these people did not believe in God's power.

Some churches I attended did believe in God's power but I never actually saw it manifest. These parishioners seemed very strange to me, yelling a lot and speaking strangely—like calling God, "God-ah!" I gave church my best shot until I couldn't take it anymore and sank deeper into despair, revisiting the occult.

A few years later I startled some psychics at the Berkeley Institute for Psychics as I was getting an aura and chakra reading. They described seeing a dark spirit in me and several more spirits hovering around. They solicited the help of a more advanced psychic. They advised me to have those dark forces leave. Well, it was not easy for me: I had tried that, but some of those spirits had been around me for years and one was my spirit guide. I left feeling down and told no one what had happened.

About a year later my sister, who had once practiced ESP and mental telepathy with me, gave her life to Jesus Christ after a series of events had transpired in her life. She telephoned me at five o'clock one morning to tell me that Jesus had awakened her and said, "Tell Doug that if he asks Me, I will remove the spirits that are on him. And tell him that I will do what is written in Deuteronomy 28—I will turn the curses in his life to blessings."

I certainly identified with the curses. I had had two cars catch fire, car batteries had exploded in my face, I was sick most of the time, and I was addicted to drugs. I remember that day with crystal clarity. I knew I had to communicate with God, and so I listened to Led Zeppelin's *Stairway to Heaven* in the hopes of getting spiritual. I pleaded with God to drive those spirits away from me, but nothing happened. But then a week later I felt the spirits leave, just as I had seven years earlier when I had started to read my Bible.

I hung out in my apartment reading my Bible for several weeks. I knew I had to go to church, yet I dreaded it. One Saturday afternoon I was reading the newspaper at a laundromat when a light seemed to shine on an ad for a denominational church I never would have chosen on my own. I checked it out and surprisingly found a group of people there who were not shocked by my spiritual experiences.

I arrived there a mess, in a "spiritual body bag." Nevertheless, over the next nine years they patiently worked with me, and I learned that I needed the fullness of the Holy Spirit to overcome what had plagued my life. I grew spiritually and learned about God's power and the gifts of the Holy Spirit. This was the first time I actually witnessed God's power being greater than Satan's power. These people showed me how to use my spiritual gifts wisely and spurred me to mature in my Christian walk.

God radically changed my life, but I never forgot what it was like to be outside the Church. It was a long, difficult adjustment to fit in to church culture. I had to learn a whole new "Christianese" language that was unintelligible to people who had not grown up steeped in "church." The sermons were often very boring, the music was outdated, and the majority of the people sat there week after week never really doing what Jesus commanded: "Go and make disciples of all nations" (Matthew 28:19).

When I expressed my disappointment and frustration about all this to a Christian friend, he responded, "That's okay, soon you'll be like us." I told him I did not want to be like them. I loved Jesus and wanted to do what was right, but I really had a hard time with the church lingo and with people not doing what Jesus did. I felt uncomfortable inviting anyone to church because it was weird to outsiders.

I considered myself one of the fortunate ones who had survived coming from the outside to be successfully integrated into the church. Many others like me couldn't do it. Some of my friends who came out of the New Age movement tried Christianity but returned within a year or two back to the New Age. Even though I did not like church services or how church people acted, I stuck with it because there was nowhere else to go. I didn't want to revert back into darkness. Yet I still hadn't encountered a church I found relevant and exciting.

Looking for Ways to Share God's Love

Because I came out of deep spiritual darkness, I immediately felt I was destined for evangelism. I wanted so badly to reach others with God's love and power, but when I talked with people about Jesus they seemed uninterested. For several years I tried nearly every evangelistic tool. I learned how to witness with a group on the streets of New York City using tracts, artwork, guitar, and other music, or whatever would capture people's attention so we could introduce them to Jesus.

Later I took James Kennedy's course called *Evangelism Explosion* and proceeded to ask people, "If you were to die tonight are you sure you would go to Heaven?" I used Bill Bright's *Four Spiritual Laws* and *Steps to Peace with God* pamphlets. I learned to share the Gospel message through a group called the Navigators by using the *Bridge to Christ* illustration, and I memorized the *Romans Road*, a series of verses from the book of Romans explaining Jesus' message.

Let me just say here that I am not putting down any evangelistic methods. We need all types of evangelistic methods and different types of churches to reach all the different types of people on earth. I honor the late Bill Bright, whose *Four Spiritual Laws* tract has been printed in over two hundred languages and been read by countless people and James Kennedy's *Evangelism Explosion*, which has for four decades successfully brought millions into a relationship with Jesus Christ.

Part of the problem is that most of our evangelistic methods and many of our church services are designed and based on principles for reaching people fifty to one hundred years ago but are just not practical today. James Kennedy's *Evangelism Explosion* organization acknowledged this in 1997 and restructured their approach to be less confrontational.

The world's societies and cultures are witnessing dramatic global changes transpiring at a feverish pace. All creation and indeed the earth itself are waiting for God's redemption, as evidenced from terrorism to tsunamis. Jesus' message doesn't need to be euphemized or made more palatable to be received by the world; we just need to communicate it with the spirit and truth of God's heart. We can be creative, relevant, and iconoclastic in sharing the "Gospel" or literally "good news." Otherwise why would people want to commit their lives to it?

My focus during my first few years as a new Christian was simply to stay alive and become more like Christ. I had so much to learn about the Bible, so many old habits to disassemble, plus I desired to become an effective evangelist. Then one day I realized that all my friends were believers, and that in my quest to be transformed through immersion in the Christian life, I had cut myself off from those who needed God's love the most. The harder I tried to reach people with the message of Jesus, the more they seemed to be trying to avoid me. I maneuvered my conversations between the tension of switching the conversation from the topics at hand to a discussion about Jesus.

I regularly witnessed to people on the streets and met formidable rejection. Deep in my gut I knew that something I was trying to convey was unnatural. I sought to be obedient, and learn, and practice the evangelistic methods popularized by Church leaders of the time. All of us faithfully did them for lack of knowing what else to do.

The rejection I encountered in my outreaches finally became unbearable, and this, along with my disillusionment with evangelistic strategies, caused me to question the destiny to which I had felt God had called me. Then I remembered reading:

> For I was hungry and you gave me something to eat, I was thirsty and you gave me something to drink, I was a stranger and you invited me in, I needed clothes and you clothed me, I was sick and you looked after me, I was in prison and you came to visit me.
> —Matthew 25:35-36

This Scripture offered me direction on conveying God's love with those in need, as Jesus said if we touch these, we are actually touching Him. From that point on, I knew I would not fulfill my divine purpose unless I began to reach out to society's outcasts.

While standing one afternoon at the Berkeley, California marina, gazing at San Francisco looming mysteriously in a bank of fog, God informed me, almost audibly, inside my mind: "I'm sending you to San Francisco to pray for the sick and minister to the homeless." I thought, *Right, I'm living fifty miles away and I have no contacts.*

Within a month I had a new job in San Francisco. Next a coworker introduced me to Sister Frye, a woman who had been running a homeless mission there for thirty-five years; my coworker told me that if I volunteered to wash dishes for a few months, Sister Frye might give me a chance to preach at one of the evening services. I had never preached a sermon in my life, but I knew God was leading me in that direction.

I walked into the mission, introduced myself to Sister Frye, and told her I was only available on Wednesday nights. She answered, "I've been praying for someone to come on Wednesday nights. Can you preach next Wednesday?" I didn't have to spend months washing dishes, though I did help in the kitchen. I preached my first sermon in October 1991 to a group of homeless people. Over the next three years I became close with these people as I ministered, played my guitar, and prayed with them.

A short time later a woman from my church approached me about writing to her friend who was on death row. I proceeded to exchange letters with him, and from this began visiting death row inmates at San Quentin prison. It seemed the abused, outcast, disenfranchised, and indigent inmates were the ones most open to hearing about God. Something happened inside me during the years I spent visiting prison inmates and praying for AIDS victims and crack addicts. I realized how much God loves everyone. I suppose I "caught" God's heart for people; I could feel Him weep over those who didn't know His love; I became sensitive to how special and important every person is to Him, no matter how insignificant one may seem to us. It was a poignant time in my life.

Meanwhile, I had become one of the most popular speakers at the homeless mission. At the same time, I was struggling in sharing God's love with my neighbors and coworkers. Then one day at my office in San Francisco, I experienced something that changed the way I viewed sharing God's love. I owned a pickup truck, which created a demand for me to move items—an automatic ministry. On a walk through the office, I overheard a homosexual coworker talking on the phone about needing to move a piece of furniture. I immediately felt the Holy Spirit prompt me to help this man. I approached his desk and volunteered to help him with my truck. "Great!" he replied. "I need to move my waterbed into my partner's house. We're moving in together this weekend." Oh, I thought, *This cannot be of God. I must not have heard the Holy Spirit correctly.* But again I felt God prod me to proceed and help him.

I drove him and his water bed over to his friend's house in the Castro district, an act that surprised him coming from a Christian. This simple act of kindness sparked a deeper friendship between us, which bore fruit a year or so later when he and his partner developed AIDS, and I was the first and only one at work that he felt comfortable confiding this to. A few years later several of our deep conversations brought peace to him before his death. That encounter taught me that friendship and kindness are powerful means to express God's love.

All You Need Is Love
A book called *Conspiracy of Kindness* by Steve Sjogren, a pastor in Cincinnati, Ohio relates how acts of kindness from him and his church were turning the city upside down. Their approach was unoffensive. Sjogren called what they were doing "servant evangelism," which he defined as deeds of love, plus words of love, plus adequate time. They

went out and gave away free sodas, or washed cars, and gave people a little card that read: I HOPE THIS BRIGHTENS YOUR DAY. IT'S OUR WAY OF SAYING GOD LOVES YOU, NO STRINGS ATTACHED.

Each time acts of kindness are done in Jesus' name, the recipients are brought a little closer to Him. How long does it take for someone to come to Christ? Sjogren claims it is a unique amount of time for each individual. As in Isaiah 55:10–11, God will not allow any seed that is sown to come back without fruit. He also states that Americans tend to view evangelism as a one-shot deal—a "let 'em have it while we've got their attention" blast from both barrels of a shotgun loaded with Scripture. Rather, Sjogren's approach is low-keyed and looks for opportunities to get into relationship with people instead of having cold encounters on the street.

Sjogren's book outlines three stages a Christian goes through in learning to share God's love: the shark, the carp, and the dolphin. In the shark stage, most Christians believe that Jesus' message must be conveyed aggressively, similar to the pattern of predatory sharks. Sharks move in for the kill without concern for the trail of bodies and debris left in their wake. They expect that if they confront enough people about receiving Jesus Christ as their personal Savior, sooner or later someone will respond affirmatively. What they don't realize is that they may be alienating more people from Christ than they are drawing to Him. The shark stage of evangelism attracts plenty of rejection, and the average person can tolerate continual rejection for only so long. Unless one is a born salesperson, the shark mode will soon utterly disillusion most people with the whole idea of sharing God's love. At this point they leave the shark mode and move on to the next stage of evangelism.

After the sharks sink to rock bottom, they become carps. Carps loiter together out of sight on the fringes. They come to the surface once in a while to hang out at church with their Christian friends, at their Christian events, but the majority of the time they bury their heads like ostriches, telling their fellow believers that evangelism is not one of their gifts. They believe Christians should share the love of God and have old war stories of being on the streets, but the pain of rejection from friends, family, and coworkers has crippled them from continuing.

The dolphin, as opposed to the shark and the carp, is more caring and sensitive to others and functions in a unique way. Dolphins learned to adapt to various situations facing them and have uncovered the secret of sharing God's love while still being true to themselves. They swim intrepidly on the surface, undaunted by the depths of the open sea. They are jubilantly playful and enjoy and excel at whatever they do. A dolphin's splash gets everyone wet (with the Spirit) but no one seems to mind in the midst of such fun. Their echolocation pinpoints just what approach will touch the need in each person so none will flounder.

Sjogren's book was my first exposure to true "outside the box" style of evangelism. I totally identified with the ideas he presented, and I consider him a genius at evangelistic teaching. On a vacation to Ohio, I visited the Vineyard in Cincinnati and experienced how to do servant evangelism firsthand. It so thrilled me that I left my full-time job to become the evangelism intern at my church. I joined a local missions team that brainstormed about new and creative ways to break through people's walls and be in ongoing relationship with them. Our ideas had practical applications to nearly every church ministry. Our bag lunches for the homeless after church on Sunday became a barbecue picnic for them with even a live band. The responses were inspiring. One guy claimed, "You washed my car every month, raked my leaves, and gave me a cold soda. I give up. I've never seen God's love demonstrated so practically; I'm here to help!"

During this time my pastor, Ben Pierce, and I developed a detailed course on friendship evangelism that was taught to hundreds of people in English and Spanish. The material we presented laid the groundwork for my work today. God has given me a deeper understanding of the principles of friendship and servant evangelism through my personal experience using them. I am keenly aware, as Romans 2:4 states, that ". . . God's kindness leads you toward repentance."

Close Encounter of a Third Kind
After finding new and exciting ways to touch people with God's love, I felt for the first time that I was beginning to touch on how Jesus did it. Although we were not seeing droves of people giving their lives to God, we were seeing some, and many new visitors graced the church. I would much rather be out serving people, or having coffee with them, and in

the process getting to know people who need God's love, than be sitting in a pew doing nothing.

In the nineties my church was starting a healing center, so I traveled with a group of leaders to the Anaheim Vineyard for a conference with John Wimber. I had heard about how John Wimber had started a movement that was restoring the power of God, in a way that was very natural, to the Church. Wimber's Association of Vineyard Churches had grown to over two hundred and fifty churches by the time of his death in 1997.

I was pleasantly surprised when I saw this man stand up in front of thousands of people dressed in a Hawaiian shirt and a pair of shorts. As he ministered, the power of the Holy Spirit would come sweeping across the crowd. People would laugh, and they even got healed just sitting in their seats! While this was happening, Wimber would casually explain what was going on as if we were in a personal teaching session.

John Wimber had written several books, but the one that interested me the most was *Power Evangelism*. He noted that whenever Jesus or His disciples proclaimed the Gospel message, a demonstration of God's power would confirm it. Evangelism in the New Testament was not telling people about God's love and then trying to reason with them to believe; it was sharing the message and then showing them God was real by performing miracles or giving words of prophecy. And this was all grounded in and accomplished through relationship, love, and acceptance of people as they were.

Wimber's message definitely followed the pattern Jesus had laid out for us by example. I remembered declaring years before I became a Christian that if I could only see God's power then I really would believe. What a way to be an evangelist! The only drawback was that I didn't know very many people who could perform miracles. I had witnessed a few healings here and there as I prayed for people, but they were paltry compared to the works described in the New Testament.

I was eager to grow in my ability to hear God's voice through the Holy Spirit. About the same time that I saw John Wimber, a friend took me to a conference with John Paul Jackson called *Hearing the Voice of God*. John Paul was known then as one of the "Kansas City prophets." He had been a part of Mike Bickle's church in the 1980s and after leaving Kansas City, John Paul was on staff with John Wimber for a few years until he pioneered and pastored a church of his own. Eventually he started a prophetic-equipping ministry called Streams Ministries International.

John Paul Jackson, who appeared to hear God clearly, intrigued me. I would watch as he called people out in a crowd and communicate a message from God that often made them cry. He did it with such gentleness, not pointing out their sins, but instead telling them how God saw them, and how they would be greatly used by God if they would not give up.

John Paul Jackson also taught on how God speaks through our dreams. I had been dreaming ever since I could remember, and no one had ever mentioned to me that as a Christian I could learn to understand my dreams. I was amazed, and as I continued for a few years attending conferences of John Paul Jackson and John Wimber, I began to grow in hearing God's voice. I became convinced that the missing ingredient in effectively witnessing for Jesus Christ was power evangelism. I began to pray and ask God to use me in this way. After all, Jesus did say "But you will receive power when the Holy Spirit comes on you; and you will be my witnesses . . ." (Acts 1:8).

A short time later something unusual happened. At the time I was a computer network engineer, and I owned my own company. I was up late working at around 11 P.M. when out of the blue a picture popped into my head of a woman who worked for one of my clients. I sensed she was in trouble, and then the word "suicide" sounded an alarm through my head. I took a moment and prayed, entreating God to save her. Then the impression left, and I continued with my work. The next day I just happened to be going to that particular client's office. I saw the woman whom I had prayed for, and suddenly the Holy Spirit strongly urged me to speak with her. But I didn't know what to say. The right moment came at break time, and at the coffeepot I awkwardly asked her how she was doing. Then I blurted out, "Last night I felt that God told me to pray for you because you may have been feeling discouraged." (That was putting it mildly!) She looked at me with tears in her eyes and affirmed that last night she had been feeling discouraged, and was drinking wine to relax. Just about 11 P.M. she had contemplated taking a handful of sleeping pills, but for some reason she stopped. Then she studied my face and asked, "Are you psychic?" "No," I replied. "I just hear God, and He must really love you to have someone pray for you like that." Soon after that incident she began attending church again.

This was the start of my series of "God encounters" over the next few years that greatly changed the way I viewed evangelism and inspired me to pursue the upward call of my destiny in God. All my life I had felt there was something more for me—that I was created for a special purpose, but I had never discovered what that something more was.

A few years later I met my wife, Linda, and I left my church and joined the Vineyard movement, where the two of us became church planters. We started and pastored a church in the Midwest, in the same area where I had once played in an occult band. After just a year of working in that church, we began reaching people in the New Age movement. We subsequently returned to California, handing the church over to a capable young pastor.

Around the same time John Paul Jackson launched the Institute for Spiritual Development courses *The Art of Hearing God* and *Understanding Dreams and Visions*.[1] During the advanced dreams course I attended, John Paul mentioned that some of his interns were using his method of biblical dream interpretation for evangelism. They were taking dream teams into Starbucks, Borders, and Barnes and Noble on a regular basis, and people were giving their lives to Jesus Christ as a result of having their dreams interpreted. When I heard this, my heart nearly skipped a beat! This is what I had dreamed of—power evangelism combined with the prophetic element of hearing God for others—a new way of sharing God's love with people who are "way outside" the Church.

I joined the staff of Streams Ministries under John Paul Jackson and became the National Dream Team Coordinator. My job was to teach people how to use dream interpretation and their prophetic gifts for evangelism. We began to take our dream and prophetic teams to events like the Olympics, the Commonwealth Games, the Sundance Film Festival, and to places like Las Vegas, Nevada; Venice Beach, California, as well as many New Age events. Streams Ministries is a vital and anointed instrument being used to restore the awe of God and to assist people in fulfilling their divine destinies.

Streams Dream Teams found that people really were more open to talking about God after they had a dream interpreted or when they received a prophetic word. In order for them to tell us their dream, they had to risk being vulnerable. As people confided in us, we gave them words of encouragement from God; we communicated spirit-to-spirit. The results were phenomenal. Over and over the Streams Dream Teams ministered to people who did not have a relationship with Jesus but were having dreams from God. Often these dreams had remained in their minds for years, but they had not been able to find anyone who could interpret them.

After two years at Streams, Linda and I felt God calling us to launch our own ministry, InLight Connection, training people in power and prophetic evangelism to reach people outside the Church.

Searching for How Jesus Evangelized
We began taking teams out to malls every week in various cities around the U.S. and observed that people were very open to talking about spirituality. They would often allow us to pray with them as long as we didn't use traditional religious words or sound churchy, but when we did, they would immediately put up their walls and quickly lose interest. If we shared words from God with them in nonreligious language, though, they seemed very interested. My intent was not just to have nice conversations with people but to see them come to know and understand God's acceptance, forgiveness, and power in their lives.

I realized I needed to familiarize myself with the culture of non-believers and to notice people's behavior and reactions when I talked to them. I had always considered common evangelistic programs outdated, so I sought to discover what people like and dislike today—their values, and what sorts of things interest them. I also began to study the Bible more deeply, researching every encounter Jesus and His disciples had with unbelievers. I was surprised to see that they did not say what we say, or use the Bible verses we use but instead demonstrated the power of God through kindness, miracles, healings, words of knowledge, prophecy, or whatever would get people to understand God's love for them.

Why I Wrote this Book

I have learned from being set free from the occult by the power of God's love, and I have learned about how to reach people with God's love. I still remember what it felt like as an unbeliever to be evangelized, yet I have also seen how the other side lives, the frustrated evangelist trying to devise ways to bring salvation to those who do not yet know God. I believe, though, that God is calling us to be creative regarding how we go about touching these people's lives. We've put parameters around an expression of spirituality that no longer fits. People today are actually more and more spiritually attuned, and they are very open to experiencing more of God.

We must discard our preconceived ideas of how to do evangelism. May this book help you find new ways to share God's good news. In these pages, my desire is to help both the seasoned evangelist as well as those who may have never dreamed they would be able to share God's love with others.

CHAPTER 2

REACHING UNREACHABLE PEOPLE

For centuries missionaries have traveled around the world to evangelize the heathens in remote places. Conversely, American church attendance is either on a decline or not growing at all. In the year 2000 roughly half of all American churches did not add one new person through conversion.[1]

Studies show that Americans over the age of eighteen have only a six percent probability of accepting Jesus Christ as their Savior.[2] Too many of those who have grown up attending church will probably stop attending once they go out on their own. It's frightening that in many cases we are not effectively reaching our own children, much less those outside the Church.

Large numbers of people do not have a relationship with Jesus Christ, and many of those who do claim to, do not grasp the meaning of the Bible. Also, they are not regularly involved in sharing their faith with others.

Many Americans consider themselves spiritually satisfied, yet contradictions and confusion permeate their lives. Their children are enrolled in church programs to learn about God; although they are loved, they are not adequately prepared for life. They do not have enough understanding of the Bible to sustain them when they establish independent lives. So despite a lot of religious activity in the United States—over sixty billion dollars is spent every year on domestic ministry and evangelism—there has not been a substantial increase in church membership in a number of years.[3]

Either this fact has passed unnoticed by most Christians, or we have become callused or complacent and believe it "doesn't get any better than this." I find it alarming that we have become content with our comfortable lives while people in our own cities are dying every day without ever experiencing a personal relationship with Jesus Christ.

We assume that the unreached people groups on the planet, classified by missionary agencies, are in Africa, China, and other faraway places. But in reality we pass them on the streets and in the grocery stores every day. They deliver our mail, or perhaps they are our children's teachers. They are everywhere! They are the people who are in need of God's love, but can't seem to find it. They are the people who are not yet reached.

Why are there people in our communities who have not been reached with God's love through Jesus Christ? It isn't because we haven't been trying, or at least tried in the past, to reach them. Many of us gave up after being rejected a few dozen times when we tried to change the topic of conversation to God. Too often we have ended up thinking people just don't want to hear about God.

There are faithful Christians who persevere at sharing God's love in spite of being rejected. They tend to use evangelistic methods appropriate forty to fifty years ago, never stopping to ponder why the people they are targeting aren't open to their attempts to share God's love. I've actually heard Christians say they believe the Gospel message is just offensive to people, and God's wrath will hold those people who reject it accountable. They cite Jeremiah 6:10–11:

> To whom can I speak and give warning? Who will listen to me? Their ears are closed so they cannot hear. The word of the LORD is offensive to them; they find no pleasure in it. But I am full of the wrath of the LORD, and I cannot hold it in.

This verse was written to the Israelites, people who believed in God but had rejected Him. It was not meant for those who are not believers, and it is not how Jesus taught us to interact with those who do not believe in Him.

Still, people need God. And how will they know about Him if we don't tell them? Our job is simply to share the message.

> How, then, can they call on the one they have not believed in? And how can they believe in the one of whom they have not heard? And how can they hear without someone preaching to them?
> —Romans 10:14

Presenting the good news of Jesus Christ to people isn't easy. Have you ever been with people and tried to veer the topic of conversation to God? Quickly a room will quiet, and the conversation's participants will raise ramparts of defense so that even if you do get to continue, their ears and hearts would have closed.

A few reasons this happens are:

1. Mentioning God makes people feel guilty because they are afraid they're doing things that don't please God. Nowadays people pay therapists wads of money in attempt to assuage their guilt.
2. They may have had an unpleasant religious experience when they were young. "I served my time in church as a child."
3. They may have had a bad experience with Christians who were rude or forceful or hypocritical about what they believed. They may have been turned off by someone's attempt to evangelize them.

"Regardless of its true character and intent, the Christian community is not known for love, nor for a life-transforming faith. . . .Outdated means of outreach, inappropriate assumptions about people's faith, and a lack of passion for helping nonbelievers to receive God's love and acceptance are hindering the Church from fulfilling its mandate."[4] With this awareness we must find new ways to communicate God's love to people in need.

Our Job Versus God's Job

When I first came into the Christian life I said, "If the message of Jesus Christ is true (which it is), you would think people would be beating down the doors of churches everywhere!" But it just isn't happening that way. Somehow Jesus' simple message has gotten complicated and even confusing to those it was most meant to reach. Simple observation should show us something isn't working right in how we convey God's love.

Once I became a Christian, I knew I needed to go to church. I figured churches were all alike, so I picked the one closest to my house for convenience's sake. I traipsed in unannounced one Sunday morning, and we were all shocked. I later realized I had to choose both how I was going to worship and what I was going to believe. I was not a mature enough Christian to understand issues like predestination, total depravity, the pretribulation rapture, Calvinism, Arminianism, or Charismatics, Pentecostals, fundamentalists, etc. "My goodness! I thought I was just giving my life to Jesus and becoming a Christian." I had no idea it was so involved.

Christians needlessly complicate Jesus' simple, straightforward message and waste precious time and energy bickering over theology or how to worship properly. We need to get back to the basics. We need to know what we believe, but these beliefs should never be allowed to become a stumbling block to others who need Jesus.

Jesus' message is actually quite simple:

- "Come follow Me . . . " (Matthew 4:19). This was one of the first things Jesus stated in His public ministry.
- "Love the Lord your God with all your heart and with all your soul and with all your mind. This is the first and greatest commandment. And the second is like it: Love your neighbor as yourself" (Matthew 22:37–39). Jesus effectively summed God's commandments up in three sentences.
- "Therefore go and make disciples of all nations, baptizing them in the name of the Father and of the Son and of the Holy Spirit, and teaching them to obey everything I have commanded you . . . " (Matthew 28:19–20). These were the last words Jesus uttered before ascending to Heaven.

Most Christians, to greater or lesser degrees, know and understand Jesus' message. Much of society in nations professing to be Christian have also been exposed to Christianity and know of Jesus, but unfortunately, many of them do not understand His message. Before I became a Christian, I thought Jesus' message was—if you are good you go to Heaven, and if you are bad you go to hell. This is simplistic, superficial, and untrue. So not only must we find new ways to communicate God's love, we have the job of working to change people's understanding of what Jesus requires of His followers. And we must do this in a fallen world that has been neither much impressed nor influenced by what they have seen or experienced of "Christianity."

With so much against us, how do we approach this monumental task? The only way to convey God's love to people hostile to God's message is through the direction of the Holy Spirit. We must understand what our part of the task is and what is God's. We have fostered guilt-based tactics of proselytization. For years I was convinced that if only people's consciences would feel conviction over sins, then everyone would repent and turn to Jesus. A popular belief among Christians is that God wants to use us to help people see their sins, and give them the choice of whether or not to receive Jesus. If we look more closely at what the Bible really declares as Jesus' message, we will have a plumb line to see just how off track we have veered with this sort of thinking.

Jesus states clearly in John 16:8 that the Holy Spirit will come and convict the world of guilt in regard to sin. God's task is to convict people of sin, and ours is to love people. "Love your neighbor as yourself" (Matthew 22:39). And when we do love people, and also love one another, they will know that we are true followers of Jesus (John 13:35).

When we use guilt-inducing methods to communicate Jesus' message, people usually respond by erecting walls and closing their minds to what we are saying, no matter how truthful it may be. On the contrary, if we treat people in a kind and loving way, they generally tend to be very open and their walls recede. It is not for us to bring them to repentance; that's the Holy Spirit's domain, and He accomplishes it much better than we ever could.

Interestingly, while for years street evangelists have employed guilt-invoking methods to cause people to realize their need for God, conversely our society has become more and more therapeutically-minded. Myriad self-help books and counselors are advising people that guilt is negative, nonproductive, and even detrimental to their health, and they need to release these feelings. Thus, guilt is not an effective means of evangelizing and it actually obscures God.

I recently had an opportunity to attend a large Hare Krishna convention on Venice Beach in California. The Krishnas were all worshipping and honoring their gods. At the end of the parade a band of irate Christians yelled at the people through a loud speaker that God was angry with them and that they must repent and turn to Jesus or they would go to hell. I was shocked that people were still around who believed that shoving the Gospel down someone's throat effectively demonstrates God's love.

In a surprising turn of events, the Krishna group circled the Christians and began showering them with rose petals and giving the peace sign with smiles on their faces. I was moved by the response of the Krishna group who loved their enemies, and I was saddened that the Christians were viewed by thousands of people as being narrow-minded, angry people. I wonder what Jesus would have said at the end of that day. "Who showed love?" I'm not saying that Krishna beliefs are correct, but we certainly don't want to alienate the very people we are endeavoring to touch and meanwhile misrepresent God's heart. For we are Jesus' ambassadors, and the world is looking at us!

Too often Christians, with every good intention, end up being the biggest obstacle to a seeker coming to Jesus Christ. Evangelistic strategies to avoid are discussed in the book *Irresistible Evangelism* by Steve Sjogren, Dave Ping, and Doug Pollock. The following "Seven Deadly Sins of Evangelism" mentioned there should be avoided.[5] They are nearly guaranteed to turn people off and prevent you from effectively sharing God's love.

Seven Deadly Sins of Evangelism

1. Scheming: Scheming evangelists use things like tracts disguised as money, phony religious surveys to get their feet in the door, and secular business or marriage seminars with unadvertised

altar calls. They also mix evangelism with fund-raising and selling of such products as vitamins and long-distance phone service.

2. Scalp Hunting: The stereotypical Scalp Hunter evangelists are religious zealots whose passion is to fill their daily quota of souls for Jesus.

3. Screaming: These preachers shout condemnation and insults at the passing crowd.

4. Selling Jesus as If He's a Juicer: These people use a highly-produced, stage-managed pitch for Jesus. They treat selling Jesus as if He's a fabulous new product guaranteed to revolutionize your life.

5. Stalking: Stalker evangelists are overzealous missionaries who just won't leave a potential target alone.

6. Sermonizing: These are the proselytizers who have all the answers—even when nobody is asking any questions.

7. Spectating: This is the deadliest of all the evangelistic sins. For whatever reason, these are simply afraid to speak up.

What People Believe They Need

Missionaries train for years, studying the culture, language, and religions of the people groups, and they translate the Bible into local dialects. If we want to reach people in our own culture who do not know Jesus Christ, we must take the task as seriously as missionaries do and aim to be missionaries in our own communities.

All people around the globe have in common the need for God. We were all created from the same blueprint. Then God said, "Let us make [humanity] in our image, in our likeness..." (Genesis 1: 26). We also know that God is Spirit (John 4:24). Since we are all created in God's likeness, we are all spiritual beings and innate within each of us from birth is a need to be in relationship with and serve our Creator. People will argue this point, but when faced with death or tragedy, there are no atheists in foxholes. Unfortunately, our understanding of God is filtered through the lens of our own experiences. If we had a cruel and controlling father, we will often believe that the nature of our heavenly Father is the same. Those who have had a bad religious experience or who grew up in church but never had a personal relationship with God, will probably not continue to be involved in a church as an adult.

We are finding as we do outreaches in coffeehouses and bookstores that many people who don't go to church or who are involved in New Age or occult practices have often grown up in a "Christian" family or attended church in their childhood. The majority have not had a positive religious experience. Jesus Himself had more confrontations with the Pharisees than with any other people group; He had his own issues with religion. Notwithstanding, no matter how we perceive Him: God is still God. His nature does not change; He is, has been, and always will be kind, loving, patient, and forgiving.

Jesus died on the cross to reconcile us to God, if we so choose. As Jesus' representatives our role is to display aspects of the divine nature that serve to draw people into relationship with their Creator. The great news is that God desires relationship even more than we do. Thus, the obligation to make disciples of all nations does not need to inspire dread and scenarios of rejection. If we change our approach to and view of the people God seeks to touch, we can ensure that we are not stumbling blocks to God's purposes for them.

We must take the time to understand—and it often may require long-suffering persistence—where people are coming from. If we seek to understand their values and perceived needs, and as much of their background and frame of reference as we can, then we will know better how to relate to them. We know they need God, but they may not be sure what they need; or they may want help solving their problems, getting love and acceptance, or locating a safe place to find out if Christianity is right for them first. Lee Strobel's book *Inside the Mind of Unchurched Harry and Mary*, although over ten years old, has some helpful information on how to relate to unbelievers. Strobel, together with Bill Hybels, is on the pastoral staff of Willow Creek Community Church that challenges churches to change their services to make seekers feel comfortable enough to visit and find out more about God. Some of Strobel's observations of unchurched people are:[6]

1. They have rejected church, but that does not necessarily mean they have rejected God.

2. They are perhaps morally adrift but secretly want an anchor.

3. They resist rules and probably authority but are very open to reasoning and learning.

4. They don't fully understand Christianity but are also unsure what they believe in.

5. They have legitimate questions about spiritual matters and expect concrete answers from Christians.

6. They don't just ask "Is Christianity true?" They often ask "Will Christianity work?"

7. They don't just want to know about something, they want to experience it.

8. They don't want to be somebody's project but would like to be somebody's friend.

9. They may distrust authority but are receptive to authentic biblical models of godly leadership. They will trust leaders who are open and accountable about personal and financial issues.

10. They are no longer loyal to denominations but are attracted to places where their needs will be met.

11. They are not particularly joiners but are hungry for a cause they can connect with.

12. Even if they are not spiritually sensitive, they want their chil-

dren to get quality moral training.

13. They are confused about gender roles but are unaware that the Bible can clarify for them what it really means to be a man or a woman.

14. They are proud that they are tolerant of different faiths but think that Christians are arrogant and narrow-minded.

15. There's a good chance they would try going to church if a friend invited them, but this may actually do them more harm than good. George Barna has found that one out of every four unchurched people would come to church at the invitation of a friend—that is fourteen to twenty million adults open to coming to church. However, if they come, they may experience the reason they left—nothing has changed.

If we seriously desire to reach people for Christ, we will have to sacrifice for outsiders to experience God's love for them.

Love, Acceptance, and Power
Every human being not only wants but needs to be loved, accepted, and to have a power greater than him- or herself to help overcome life's troubles. Many people have felt unaccepted in traditional religious settings and want a God who has real power—not only in the macrocosm of the world at large but in their own lives. They need a God who is omniscient, omnipotent, and omnipresent not only for historical figures of Scripture but One who can identify with their pain while bringing them a higher, more abundant life here and now.

As we learn to display God's love to the unlovable and His acceptance to the outcasts, we will see divine intervention in people's lives. We must allow people the same freedom the Holy Spirit gives us—freedom of choice—and time to feel comfortable in a Christian community, without passing judgment on them. There's incredible power in the simple act of unconditional love and acceptance. Jesus demonstrated this repeatedly by His works among the nonreligious multitude.

It's fine to talk about allowing the unlovable, the social outcasts, and the unbelievers into our churches but not so easy to do. I was pastoring a church that was attempting to do exactly this in a town with many New Age adherents. One day I received a telephone call from a local psychic who claimed she was trying to find a church that would let her come and find out more about Jesus. I was not surprised that several pastors had told her not to come to their churches until she stopped doing tarot card readings. I invited her to come to our service, and afterward she told me she had had a dream that she was sleeping by a well and Jesus walked up to her. I asked her if she had ever read the book of John in the New Testament and she said no, she had not. In John 4, Jesus spoke to a Samaritan woman at a well. I felt this was a strong indication that God was drawing this woman to Himself.

As my wife and I began to form relationships with people and loved them unconditionally, we began taking "field trips" to underground clubs, smoky New Age coffeehouses, and weird art shows. We genuinely made friends and cared for people. It took a little time and was messy, but some of the strangest people began to come to know Jesus' love and acceptance for them. Next they would invite their strange friends, who in turn invited their strange friends. We were watching people meet Jesus who were by far the least likely candidates—at least by human standards. When you are truly accepting and loving to outcasts, and invite them into your church, you will often have to deal with the attitudes of people from other churches in your community. They will not understand what you are doing and will determine you are a cult. Well, people didn't understand Jesus either, and thought He and His disciples were a cult. . . and worse.

Study the Culture
To reach people in our communities, we must go to the places where they are. I have spent the past few years traveling around the U.S. leading outreach teams in hundreds of malls, bookstores, and coffee shops. In a sense we were doing a demographic study of people in the major cities of America. We talked with people, watched them, prayed with them, and were very surprised to find that people are very open to spirituality.

Try walking around your city looking for places people like to hang out. Most often it's Starbucks, Jamba Juice, Borders Bookstores, or Barnes and Noble. These establishments not only sell their products but they offer a communitylike atmosphere where you are free to sit, chat, and drink beverages. They also offer monthly events and discussion groups that include a number of spiritual topics such as meditation, tarot card readings, and astrology study groups. These stores are not out to promote occult teachings; they have simply ascertained and are providing what they feel their clientele value—in order to increase their sales.

We can learn a good deal about people's felt needs in our area by reading the events calendars at the bookstores. This realization prompted me to initiate similar events and to get our groups added to various calendars. To reach the community we must become part of the community.

Speak the Language
For many the prospect of attending a church for the first time is overwhelming. Not only are these new disciples contemplating a relationship with God but they are facing an alien subculture with a strange language. Christians have unthinkingly developed "insider" phrases with words unused in everyday work or school life. In order to communicate effectively about God with ordinary people who do not have a religious background, we must learn to speak in a way they can understand.

Words and phrases such as *mantle, call of God, anointing, God placed you on my heart*, are only understood by people who know the Bible. This is a foreign language to unchurched people. There are simple ways to rephrase this commonly used Christianese language so people outside the Church can understand what we mean. Our tendency is to want to sound religious. The phrase *God placed you on my heart* could be more easily understood if rephrased as *I have been thinking about you lately*. The meaning is actually identical. *You have a call of God on your life* can be reworded *Your life has destiny*! I will discuss the subject of learning to speak using nonreligious language in more detail in Chapter Five.

Modern Parables
One of the main ways Jesus communicated God's message was through parables—fictional stories that illustrate parallel truths. Jesus often would teach "The Kingdom of Heaven is like . . . ." Sometimes He depicted it as a man planting seed in his field or like yeast in dough.

Other times He described the Kingdom of Heaven as treasure hidden in a field or a king preparing a wedding reception for his son.[7]

The parables Jesus narrated were easy to grasp. The people of His day understood the analogies to farming, cooking, and kings. Somehow in the twenty-first century, though, people don't catch His meaning as easily and clearly because of the difference in cultures. If Jesus were alive today, I believe He would still speak in parables, but His parables would involve the elements of our everyday life.

One of the most effective means of making spiritual comparisons is to use popular movie themes as parables. For instance, in the film *The Matrix*, the character Neo is the prophesied "Chosen One" who will liberate the people and overthrow the machines. This is a great parallel to the Bible's prophecy of a coming "Chosen One" who will liberate people from the oppression of sin and overthrow the rule of Satan. That Chosen One has come, and His name is Jesus Christ. In giving the Gospel message to someone without a religious background it would be easy to tell them that Jesus is like Neo.

My ministry requires that I travel around the country and lead prophetic teams on outreaches into malls. I have trouble explaining what I do to nonbelievers, and especially to my family members. The best way I have to explain it is to tell people that what I do is similar to the movie *Minority Report*. In the movie there are "Pre-Cogs" who get visions of the future and stop crimes before they happen. One of the Pre-Cogs, Agatha, is taken to a mall; she stops a woman and insists, "Don't go home. He knows." This is similar to what we do when we go to the malls; we tell people messages from God about themselves, focusing on the positive side.

The Lord of the Rings trilogy is full of spiritual metaphors. *Forrest Gump* is a great example of humility. *The Postman*, *Saving Private Ryan*, *Citizen Kane*, even episodes from *The Beverly Hillbillies* can be used to explain principles of God. People enjoy movies, and the multimedia approach is the way most in our society are accustomed to learning. Therefore, it's important to use multimedia presentations whenever possible during church services. Many books and websites are available that elaborate on this subject. We do need to be careful what we watch, but often God will use a movie to speak to people about their spiritual condition.

Building Relationships

The most basic way to reach people who don't know God loves them is to get to know them and get involved in their lives. I inform our teams that most people are not going to be interested in discussing eternal issues when we don't even know the names of their children or their pets. We must get to know them as friends. We need to be in relationships with unchurched people—not view them as our evangelistic project—because they truly matter to God.

Relationship-based evangelism is the most effective means of helping someone come to know and understand God's love for them. Our teams have found that many people, even in the New Age movement, are pleasantly surprised to come across Christians who are willing to talk openly with them. They are surprised if you are willing to listen because they are so used to having one-sided conversations with believers who only tell others what they need. If we listen, then they will listen to us. People value meaningful conversation and like to explore various views.

I really enjoy the company of friends who will genuinely listen to me when I am in need. But being a good listener is not a skill that comes automatically. To learn to listen to others, I took a course called *Listening for Heaven's Sake* that teaches you how to genuinely listen to people.[8] People feel valued when you listen to them. And when you are truly listening, then you will know how to appropriately respond in order to serve. Remember: "A word aptly spoken is like apples of gold in settings of silver" (Proverbs 25:11).

CHAPTER
3

A LIFESTYLE
of SHARING
GOD'S LOVE

I t was a late summer evening, and I was with some friends sitting around a fountain in a neighborhood known for its bars and drugs. Hordes of people were milling around, and we were there to offer dream interpretations and encouraging words from God. Since we take a different approach and don't use tracts or Bibles in our outreaches, we were successfully engaged in blending in with the crowd.

A street evangelist approached me. He began to confront me with my need for Jesus. Before I could tell him I was a Christian, he was imposing his testimony upon me. Since he didn't seem to care whether or not I was listening, I decided to stay quiet and observe what an unbeliever on the street might feel when approached by Christians.

The evangelist continued talking. I noticed that we were now surrounded by other street evangelists. One had a suit on and was shouting, "Today is the day of salvation, and sinners must repent!"

Needless to say, the people we had been talking to and interpreting dreams for had all dispersed—running to escape the evangelists. Finally I told the outspoken street evangelists that we were Christians, but they did not believe us and proceeded to try to argue doctrine with us.

We moved up the street with the people and resumed our outreach.

I came away from this encounter feeling sorry for those whom the evangelist had chased off. Even though I was a Christian, it was difficult to experience an obnoxious approach to evangelism. Imagine being one of those people on the street, trying to understand why God was angry with you. It felt more like it was the Christians who were angry, not God.

I was shocked to learn that this style of evangelism still occurs daily in cities across America. Not only does it turn people off and drive them away from the good news of Jesus, but it gives the good news a bad name. People begin to associate Christianity with such negative encounters, when in reality God is love.

One of the biggest turning points in my Christian life came when I realized that God is deeply compassionate and that He passionately loves people who don't know Him. Translated into Christianese you could say "I got God's heart for the lost." I realized that to reach people, it's important to be sensitive and realize that the lost don't like to be called "lost." We will have better success with them if we can get out of the habit of calling them "poor, lost souls" and simply refer to them as people who need God's love.

To have God's heart for people means that we must deeply care for them and portray God's love to them. Jesus demonstrated this for us as He hung out with the sinners and outcasts of the religious society. He dined with the tax collectors (Mark 2:15–16 and Luke 19:1–10) and invited their sinful friends to join Him. On one occasion a woman who had lived a sinful life gave Him a foot massage (Luke 7:37–48), and although the religious people were offended, Jesus had compassion on her and forgave all her sins.

In order to love people the way Jesus did, we must first receive God's love and acceptance ourselves. We can't give away what we don't have. When we develop a deep intimacy with God, our love and intimacy will automatically become contagious to those around us.

For people to want the good news of Jesus, it must really be good! If God has truly changed our lives, it will show. People around us will want what we have without us begging them to receive it. Have you ever been around people who have God's presence in their lives? It permeates everything around them. They are not just being good and playing church—they've found their destiny in life.

Too often the average Christian tends to blend into the woodwork. At work one day a Christian coworker said: "I think another Christian is working here now, because I just saw a fish emblem on someone's car." Intrigued, I approached the car owner and mentioned the Christian emblem on his car. I asked if he was a Christian. He laughed and answered, "No, but I guess my car is." He had just bought the car from a Christian and wasn't sure what the fish emblem meant. I thought to myself, *It's sad that we have to look at bumper stickers to find out whether someone is a Christian.*

Christians don't stand out as being different in other ways either. Studies have shown that overall thirty-three percent of all born-again individuals who have been married have gone through a divorce, which is statistically comparable to the thirty-four percent incidence among non-born-again adults.[1]

People's faith affects some aspects of their behavior, but not all of it, according to a survey released by the Barna Research Group (Ventura, California). Survey respondents were asked to react to a half-dozen behaviors related to moral choices. There was no difference between born-again and non-born-again adults with regard to reading a magazine or watching a movie or video that contained explicit sexual images. There was no difference evident when it came to the likelihood of viewing adult-only content on the Internet or discussing a specific moral issue. Of the six behaviors related to technology use, entertainment, and lifestyle (using the Internet, using e-mail for nonemployment purposes, attending a class, recycling, reading a book for pleasure, and reading their horoscope), none elicited a difference between Christians and non-Christian adults.[2] One can only wonder if we are the lukewarm Laodicean church John referred to in Revelation 3:16. What sets us apart from those who have not turned their lives over to Jesus?

Is being a Christian really worth enough to induce people to give up their wild party lifestyle? Or their pleasures and possessions they value more than God? Yes! If we truly love God, our relationship with Him will be important to us and we'll want to spend time with Him; not because *we have to* but because we *want* to. If I asked my daughter to hang out at Starbucks with me and she replied, "Gee, Dad, I really don't want to but if you tell me to, I will," that wouldn't be a real or satisfying expression of love for me. A true loving relationship says, "Yes, I want to spend time with you because I really do love you!" Such a relationship has achieved intimacy. Our heavenly Father desires the same intimacy with us. We shouldn't feel obliged to, but it should be our fervent desire. That's why He gives us the freedom of choice; love under compulsion won't satisfy Him . . . and it won't satisfy us.

As we draw closer to God by spending time in prayer, reading the Bible, and worshipping Him, we develop deeper character. Character is the evidence of a changed life. The apostle Paul outlined some characteristics of a Christian who lives by the Spirit's power: "But the fruit of the Spirit is love, joy, peace, patience, kindness, goodness, faithfulness, gentleness and self-control. . . " (Galatians 5:22–23).

When we live our lives each day walking close to God, with His Spirit and presence around us, people will ask: "What's different about you?" It's not just our more abundant lives—it is the sense of peace, security, and love that emanates from us. If God has changed us, we will naturally want to help others change too!

The Great Commission
Many Christians feel that we must share the good news of Jesus because Jesus commanded us to. When I first gave my life to Jesus Christ, I was told that all Christians must evangelize. Before He ascended to Heaven, Jesus Himself gave us these marching orders, often referred to as "The Great Commission: "Therefore go and make disciples of all nations, baptizing them in the name of the Father and of the Son and of the Holy Spirit" (Matthew 28:19). In assessing our progress, however, several writers have called this passage "The Great Omission." We know we are all called to go and make disciples, but most of us for one reason or another don't. So once a year, pastors pull out the "We All Must Evangelize" sermon, and we develop enough guilt to go out and invite someone to church. However, anything driven by guilt won't last long. Soon we forget about evangelizing and settle back down into our spiritual inactivity, hoping no one notices. Jesus understood our tendency to act this way.

As I examined these verses more closely, I noticed something interesting. Since the New Testament was originally written in Greek, and one Greek word can have several different English meanings, I decided to look up some root meanings. The word for "go" in Greek is *poreuo-mai*, which can be translated "as you go on your journey" or "while you travel." What Jesus was actually saying is "As you go on your journey, teach people what I taught you." He was instructing us to mentor people while we go about our everyday lives, to incorporate discipleship as part of our lifestyle.

With that understanding in mind, we can then go about our business and freely share the good news of Jesus not because we have to but because of what He has done in our lives. Besides, people know when you're evangelizing them, and no one wants to be an evangelistic project or the target of a modern-day crusade. Sharing God's love must flow out of our sincere love and compassion for a person. We must be willing to walk with them through their process to salvation. When our efforts to share how God has changed us are genuine, then people will respond.

What Happened to Evangelism?
Several years ago I was part of a growing young church that met in a VFW hall on a street lined with bars. One night an evangelist came to our church for a conference. After the service the evangelist inquired if we would be willing to break into teams and go to the bars to see if God spotlighted anyone for us to encourage. We were instructed not to take tracts or Bibles. Instead we were advised to strike up conversations and, if the person was open, to offer to pray about anything they wanted.

My team entered a dark, dank, smoky bar—an environment I had been all too familiar with earlier in my life. We bought sodas and began playing pool and video games with the patrons. Within an hour we had prayed with nearly everyone in the bar. The bartender ordered pizza for us, and a member of our worship team grabbed his sax and began to jam with the jukebox. It turned out that in this bar beside our church were four backslidden Christians who had lost hope in life. As we departed, they hugged us, and some tearfully begged us to return soon. That particular event changed our attitude toward our neighborhood. It also changed the neighborhood's opinion of Christians from "those church people" to "those people who care." Our eyes need to notice the needs of people around us. In Jesus' words, "I tell you, open your eyes and look at the fields! They are ripe for harvest" (John 4:35–46).

I believe most Christians sincerely would like to touch those who don't yet know God, and their efforts at evangelism are full of good intentions. Unfortunately, though, and most importantly, Christianity and the church experience have not remained relevant to people seeking God. Numerous scandals implicating church leaders in sexual abuse and child molestation crimes have made outsiders even more leery. God is allowing these cases to come to light now and is cleaning up both the church leadership and its members to prepare us for a coming revival. We can't control the behavior of such men and women of God who have abused their positions, but we can work on being relevant and relating to people outside the Church.

We have the best message on the planet; we have the power and the Spirit of the living God. We just need to change our evangelistic focus, and get out into the community where the people who need our message of the good news are. While many of our churches continue to serve their members faithfully, all too often people right outside the church doors are dying without ever knowing God's love. Church members are unaware of the needs of the people in their own communities, so it's no wonder church growth has been at a standstill.

When I first started out in ministry I was very excited to get out and reach people, while being simultaneously bewildered at the response of my fellow Christian friends, who did not share my zeal. To me it was a no-brainer: We simply needed to look around and find out what people valued and then tailor our approach and church service to their needs. When we managed to accomplish this, we had great evangelistic success.

As I began teaching on evangelism at various churches, I noticed there seemed to be a standard, popular way to do evangelism. If we didn't do evangelism a particular way, it wasn't right. I began to try new methods and experiment outside the norm; in response often Christians would tell me I was watering down or compromising the Gospel message. This propelled me to study evangelism.

I was surprised to find that many of the popular evangelistic methods were not even in the Bible. Nowhere in the Bible did Jesus or His disciples approach people with the verses we use. When Jesus declared, "I am the way and the truth and the life. No one comes to the Father except through me," (John 14:6), he was comforting and encouraging Thomas and some of His other disciples. He never would have said anything like this verse to the Samaritan woman at the well.

Jesus called people to repent (Matthew 4:17) and Peter invited people to repent at Pentecost (Acts 2:38), but the model we use for an altar call is not in the Bible. The popular "sinner's prayer" Christians use to lead people to Jesus is not in the Bible either. These practices aren't wrong—and God has used them to help people come to Him—but they are not the *only* way or even the most effective way to minister today.

I know of a church that baptized fifteen new believers with no previous church background. The church never once had a public altar call for people to receive Jesus as their Savior. These people were led to Jesus by church members developing relationships with them and inviting them to small group meetings. When the pastor didn't include an altar call in the service, some members were so angry they left and went to another church. If we hold on tight to a traditional church model or method, we might be blinded to other methods God wants us to employ to reach millions of people.

Based on my research and observations while visiting and ministering in churches across the United States, Canada, and the United Kingdom, I have found three main factors that can negatively affect the success of evangelism. The first is emphasizing program-based church activity over Spirit-led services. Program-based church activity can often replace the need for God's power yet it offers well-refined programs. The second factor is the introduction of mass evangelism as the primary method of reaching people for Jesus. Mass evangelism makes salvation and spiritual growth an event instead of a step-by-step process in a person's life. Most people tend to come to Jesus Christ through a process of circumstances as the Holy Spirit draws them. The third factor that can affect evangelistic effectiveness is emphasizing the decision a person makes to follow Jesus as the main focus of evangelism. This decision is actually the last step in the process; it's the end result of a series of encounters and events orchestrated by the Holy Spirit. It does not stop there; it is also the first step one takes in a new life in Christ.

Programs Versus Spirit-Led Services

Churches have become more and more secular in their thinking. This has happened slowly over the last few hundred years as reliance on logic and reason, and then technology have influenced much of the Western mind-set. The result is that we tend to try to use the natural realm to explain a supernatural phenomenon. Over-emphasis on logic and natural, linear understanding can hinder our faith and belief in Jesus' words: ". . . with man this is impossible, but with God all things are possible" (Matthew 19:26).

Unbelief can insidiously enter our minds before we even realize it. That is why it's so important for us to look to God in every situation. We must welcome and make room for God's miracles and transformative power both in our lives and in our churches. Unfortunately, churches often get overly involved with programs, whose importance begins to supplant the need for God's Holy Spirit. If you've ever been to church, you know what I mean by church programs—the course-of-the-month or possibly a new seminar to learn how to better live the Christian life. It's not that programs are bad, because they are not; many people are changed through church programs. Discipleship classes, for instance, are necessary to help new believers mature in their faith. But we cannot allow our programs to replace the need for the power and presence of God's Holy Spirit. Ultimately, it is God's Spirit—not a program—that will change people.

Different types of churches exist because there are different kinds of people. One church will not fit every person. Some churches were established to allow the Holy Spirit's gifts as an active part of their worship services; these are now becoming more sensitive to visitors and less open to the manifestation of God's power. The pendulum can swing too far in either direction.

All churches should be sensitive to visitors at their services. Nevertheless, there is a way to allow room for the gifts of the Holy Spirit. I have pastored a church that reconciled the two and have since visited several others that are successfully using similar techniques to make visitors feel welcome without hindering or offending the Holy Spirit's work. Unusual manifestations are simply explained as they are occurring.

One night I was speaking about God's power to heal, and God's presence in the room was apparent. I called people forward for prayer, and the Holy Spirit touched a woman while our ministry team prayed for her. She began to cry, shake, and laugh all at the same time. It was unusual but still a legitimate touch from God. When I noticed people staring, I asked if they knew what was happening. A young man raised his hand and answered, "Sure, that's an exorcism." I simply explained: "No, it is God's Holy Spirit touching her deeply." Everyone seemed relieved, and no one was upset or left the church. In fact, they began to invite their friends to come to church, because the reality of God's power they had witnessed brought them great hope.

Whenever God's power is present, there is a good chance things will appear chaotic. On the day of Pentecost, for example, there was a lot of power and what looked like a lot of chaos (Acts 2). Many charismatic churches have begun to pull away from allowing God's miraculous power in their services because of the chaos that can happen when God begins healing people and pouring out various gifts and manifestations of His Spirit.

Once I was part of a large denominational church whose favorite Scripture was 1 Corinthians 14:40, "Let all things be done decently and in order." My response was "Notice, it says 'let all things be done.' " In other words, we can allow for the move of the Holy Spirit and still maintain order.

Most Christians agree that God can touch and heal people today, but they are concerned about things getting out of hand during a service. Yet if we try to keep a lid on God's power, the result can be that we will become more program-oriented. As the Holy Spirit begins to move in people's lives drawing them to God and awakening them spiritually, they will often come to a church looking for solutions to their out-of-control lives. In many cases, they are looking for a God with real power. In limiting God's power in the Church, we can actually cause a dilemma. We don't want to frighten such individuals away, but we want them to get the power of God they are looking for. God often uses circumstances, tragedy, and life-challenging events to draw people to Himself. Since we are all created in God's image, all people have an instinct to worship their Creator. When we remove or limit God's manifest power, we are creating a vacuum in people that must be filled. If they happen to go to a church that does not make room for God's power, most people without a religious upbringing will leave and continue their search for the power they are looking for. Often they end up with the counterfeit of this power in the New Age movement, occult groups, or heretical cults.

After getting to know people who have legitimately tried to integrate themselves into churches but found only lifeless programs, I am convinced that in some cases these churches are responsible for those who turn away from Christianity to the New Age or other spiritual groups. I believe God will hold us accountable for this injustice. Compelled by this thought, I go out of my way to reach people in the New Age movement. When we replace God's life-changing power with programs and services, we are removing the very element that brought three thousand people to Jesus in one day (Acts 2:40).

Mass Evangelism

In recent years mass evangelism has become the most popular evangelistic method and has helped bring millions of people to Jesus Christ. Many accounts of mass evangelism occur in the Bible, but each account went hand in hand with one-on-one personal relationships. Jesus taught large crowds about the Kingdom of God (Matthew 4:25), and the more popular Jesus became, the larger the crowds grew (Matthew 13:1–9). He responded by sending out smaller teams to minister personally to people in His name (Luke 10:1).

On the day of Pentecost, Peter preached to thousands of people in Jerusalem (Acts 2:41). Paul and Barnabas also spoke to a large number of people in Antioch (Acts 13:44), and in many other places as recorded in the book of Acts. Paul did not rely on large gatherings alone to evangelize; he also spoke from house to house (Acts 20:20). Mass evangelism was used in the New Testament to launch the Church, but as time went on, it seemed to taper off to more personal encounters.

In the nineteenth century a new wave of mass evangelism was seen in the campaigns of Charles Finney and D. L. Moody.[3] Both Finney and Moody worked with local clergy whose church members were allowed to participate in these outreaches. The most modern explosion of mass evangelism came in the twentieth century with Billy Sunday and Billy Graham. Sunday was the first major evangelist to use decision follow-up cards as a means of helping new believers get plugged into a local church and, thereby, be discipled.

Billy Graham was best known for bringing citywide crusades to America. Decades ago these campaigns effectively reached millions of people, but they've since lost their cutting edge. Billy Graham popularized the evangelistic style of inviting people to come forward to dedicate their lives to Jesus Christ. He also developed the famous "sinner's prayer" that most Christians have learned to use when leading someone to give his or her life to Jesus.

Billy Graham's style of mass evangelism soon became the standard method of Sunday service evangelism in churches worldwide, whether crowds were big or small. On a typical Sunday morning, the service closes with a "call for salvation," or an "altar call," in which the pastor invites those interested in receiving Jesus as their Savior to raise their hand and then come forward for prayer and repentance. In our changing society, people are no longer responding to this type of call as earlier generations did. Nowadays raising a hand in response to a salvation call may be responding more out of curiosity—indicating "Yes, I'd like more information on this subject"—than a wholehearted commitment. Despite all the raised hands, no corresponding increase in church attendance has taken place. A re-evaluation of our methods of Sunday morning evangelism is necessary, for we may be communicating inadvertently to people that "all you have to do is pray the sinner's prayer, and you won't have to go to hell." This is certainly not what churches have intended.

On the other hand, people are more likely to dedicate their lives to Jesus Christ, become true disciples, and become part of a church after developing relationships with other Christians. This relationship provides opportunities for these seekers to ask plenty of questions and to see God's love and power demonstrated in practical ways. Furthermore, such relationship building works much better in small groups than in large meetings. A good example is the success of the Alpha Courses.[4]

The Alpha Course consists of a series of talks addressing key issues relating to the Christian faith. By sharing a light meal together at the beginning of each session, people are given a chance to get to know one another. After each talk individuals are divided into small groups to discuss the topic of the evening and are given an opportunity to ask questions and express opinions. Alpha focuses on effective ways to reach people nowadays, offering coffee, small groups, listening, learning, and discovering God's truth at a more personal level and at one's own pace. Seekers can ask questions—no question is too simple or too hostile.

I'm sure we can discover many new ways to communicate the message of a new life through Jesus. We need a variety of different methods of evangelism to reach a variety of different people.

Decision-Based Evangelism

Along with mass evangelism came decision-based evangelism. During the Frontier/Revivalist movement of the 1700s, preaching had only one goal in mind: to convert souls.[5]

As I mentioned earlier, mass evangelism crusades were geared to having people respond to an altar call and then sign a decision card. The altar call became popular in churches, as did the practice of asking people to make a decision for Jesus Christ, whether at church or on the street.

Guiding people toward deciding to give their lives to Jesus Christ is the starting point for making new disciples. The New Testament shows people making a decision to follow Jesus (Acts 17:1–4). However, we need to be careful not to measure our evangelistic success by how many decisions for Christ were gained on a particular outreach.

Somewhere along the way, Christians began to believe if they persuaded a person to pray the sinner's prayer then that person was saved, regardless of whether or not the person became a disciple. Praying the sinner's prayer will only change a person's life if that person is serious about making a commitment to Jesus. The newly converted individual must then be discipled by integration into a church. These decision-based evangelistic methods may indeed produce some legitimate converts to Christianity, but overall this method may be causing more harm than good. If people praying the prayer are not truly convicted of their sin and are praying just to escape the punishment of hell, then they probably will never move forward to maturity.

Some people who have prayed for salvation and asked Jesus into their lives have never done anything to learn more about the Christian life. Therefore, they are unable to mature and mistakenly believe they have done what it takes to get into Heaven. Such people become inoculated with the Gospel message; they receive just a little of it, but not enough to bring lasting change to their lives.

Many people have prayed the sinner's prayer numerous times. Because they did it once and didn't see any change in their lives or weren't sure it "took," they repeat the process again and again. In some cases, this repetition actually reinforces their false belief that they must get resaved every time they sin. This does not mean we should stop asking people to receive Jesus Christ as their Savior.

Jesus told a parable about scattering seed. Some fell on hard ground where they would not take root and grow; some fell on good soil and grew, producing other plants and more seeds (Matthew 13:3–23). It is crucial that we learn to recognize if a person has truly made a decision to receive Jesus and plans to learn what is necessary to grow to maturity or that right time has not yet arrived and more fertilization is required.

Decision-based evangelism has become out of balance in the following areas:

1. The focus is on the number of decisions to follow Jesus instead of making new disciples. Decisions do not make disciples. Forty to fifty years ago more people had a memory of Christian teachings, or were raised in a family with Christian principles, and society's mores were more steeped in biblical standards. Therefore, getting people to make a decision to follow Jesus was actually restoring them to their godly heritage. Since today that heritage no longer permeates our culture's morality and for many people has been lost, thus it is *not* as likely to happen this way. We would do better to avoid the success-driven attitude.

2. Too much emphasis is placed on receiving Jesus as the end result of any evangelism. In reality, receiving Jesus is just the beginning of a new spiritual life. This life will require nurturing, guidance, and friendship as a means of being transformed to Christlikeness. Coming to Jesus is a process rather than a one-time event.

3. Greater sensitivity and discernment are required regarding where people are in their process of coming to Jesus. Conversations need to be geared so those in the crucible of decision will understand what is being said. Often evangelism follows a "cookie-cutter," one-size-fits-all format. To reach people effectively we must realize that each person will require a different approach.

4. Those engaging in evangelism need to understand that it is neither necessary nor productive to ask every person, in every encounter, whether they want to receive Jesus Christ as Savior. And Jesus' name does not need to be mentioned in every conversation either. Many would-be evangelists have been taught that if they don't at least attempt to lead someone to Jesus in every conversation, they are compromising the Gospel or if they are unable to have someone pray the sinner's prayer, then they have failed. This is far from the truth, and such beliefs causes us to come on too strong and often be too forceful.

Many churches and many Christians have boasted of thousands of decisions for Jesus in their evangelistic outreaches. But in many cases not one of these new converts makes it into a local church. Yet for some reason we still erroneously think this convention is the only way to make disciples even though it has not been effective for years.

Let me reiterate: I am enthusiastic about leading people to Jesus Christ, but it must be when such individuals are ready to make that all-important decision with their whole heart. When I run into people whom God has been working on, often they ask what to do next in life. These are the ones who will be most likely to become established in a local church and who will grow to maturity. In Chapter Five, I will go into greater detail about understanding evangelism as a process.

4

DOING WHAT JESUS DID— EVANGELISM *in the* NEW TESTAMENT

When I first became a Christian, I was told to read the Bible every day, pray, and memorize some verses to help me explain Jesus' message to other people. It is a good idea for all Christians to know these basics: how to explain salvation through Jesus Christ, how to lead someone in a prayer of forgiveness for one's sins, and how to assist that person in turning control of his or her life over to God.

Some people may think I am opposed to these evangelistic methods; this is far from the truth. By all means, we need to find the people who are ready and open for a life-transforming conversion experience, and we must lead them to Jesus. My concern, however, is with the underlying assumptions of the approaches most would-be evangelists use to share their faith: that everyone is ready *now* to hear the Gospel message and to repent.

Learning to lead someone to salvation is a necessity, but using the illustrated guidelines as a standard on people we have just met does not tend to be a good icebreaker. We must learn to be spiritually sensitive to where individuals are in their journey to God.

As mentioned earlier, I have tried nearly every evangelistic method

I could find. Many popular methods were effective when first developed, but were perhaps specific to a particular time or people.

In Chapter One, I mentioned the method of Evangelism Explosion (EE)[2] that uses two questions designed to determine whether people are open to talking more about their need for God. This method was very successful in the late sixties and seventies during the Vietnam War. It dovetailed with the revival called the Jesus People movement, when many disillusioned hippies began giving their lives to Jesus. During the sixties protest era, it was common to see people with clipboards on the streets gathering signatures for petitions and taking surveys, so the EE approach of asking questions seemed to fit the times.

Nowadays people are more leery of being questioned on the street. The EE approach still works for some people, but it doesn't have the widespread impact it once had, as EE's founder, James Kennedy, acknowledged in 1997, deeming it too confrontational and requiring revision in order to meet the needs of people in the twenty-first century.[3]

Many other methods of sharing Jesus Christ with people exist. Most focus on key points of the Gospel message and then invite people to pray to receive Jesus Christ as their Savior. Two of the more popular methods include using Gospel tracts developed by the late Bill Bright's *Four Spiritual Laws* and Billy Graham's *Steps to Peace with God*. These tools have been used quite effectively in the past and brought millions of people to Jesus Christ. Gospel tracts have long been the most popular method of sharing Jesus' message. Today, however, they are not as successful as they once were.

I was given so many tracts before I became a Christian that I became immune to them. People left tracts on my desk at work, handed them to me on the streets, and even put them on the windshield of my car. Once during a difficult time in my life when I remember thinking that I was hurting really bad I just wished one of these Christians would come talk to me personally, without judging me. Most Christians I met would tell me I was going to go to hell, or they would call and bug me in a harassing way. My experience made me conclude there were two kinds of Christians—the ones who were too afraid to talk with me, and the rest who were too aggressive. The latter ones, I wanted to avoid at all costs.

Tracts and many of the popular cold-approach methods of evangelism have become clichés and material for television comedians. These methods have lost momentum because the culture has changed, or perhaps they have been so overused that their intended targets are now immune to them. I often take a survey at my workshops of a show of hands from those who came to Jesus Christ after being handed a tract; to date only three people have ever raised their hands. Certainly God can use these methods to reach people, but they don't reach the masses.

Michael's Story

Although tracts are *not* the most effective means of reaching people, there are times however, when they work very well. In the case of Michael B., for instance, God used a tract to bring him into the Kingdom, and to save his life. Here's Michael's story:

I remember reaching a stage in my life when I sincerely believed there was no hope left. I saw nothing but pain in my future. The more pain I felt, the more drugs I did. Then one day I completely lost hope for life. That was it. I was determined to commit suicide. I decided to jump to my death, and I chose a window that was high enough above the ground to ensure I wouldn't survive the fall.

It was the most dramatic day of my life. As I walked around the city that night, I took a deeper, more concentrated look at the world. *This is the last time I'm going to see this,* I told myself.

What do I have to lose? I asked myself. I began to pray, asking God for meaning. I asked God to give me a sign that He wanted me to live. It was a radical prayer; I had lost almost all hope. The only hope I had left was that maybe God loved me and would answer my prayer and give me a sign. I was serious about suicide, and God knew it.

He answered my prayer. A little over sixty seconds after my request, a stranger handed me a Christian pamphlet. If the pamphlet had been given to me five or ten minutes after my prayer, I don't think I would have accepted it as a sign from God. As it turned out, I truly believe it was a miracle.[4]

Michael's story was a true miracle. God will use our efforts to reach people with His love. However, we are seeing fewer and fewer of these stories nowadays. In order to reach the billions of people who need Jesus, we must continue to search for new, creative ways to share His wonderful message.

Searching for a New Way

When it comes to evangelism, most people feel they have heard it all. "Oh, no, another new method? That means someone has taken an old method and retooled it." I used to feel this way and wondered whether there really could be a new way to do evangelism. The Bible does say nothing is new, because basically everything has been done before.

> What has been will be again,
> what has been done will be done again;
> there is nothing new under the sun.
> Is there anything of which one can say,
> "Look! This is something new"?
> It was here already, long ago;
> It was here before our time.
> —Ecclesiastes 1:9–10

But remember, the Bible also says God is always doing something new!

> "Forget the former things;
> do not dwell on the past.
> See, I am doing a new thing!
> Now it springs up; do you not perceive it?
> I am making a way in the desert
> and streams in the wasteland."
> —Isaiah 43:18–19

I believe God is saying to us: "Don't let the past limit the future." We can use the past to help us learn and move forward. So I have continued to explore new evangelistic methods and faithfully try to share God's love whenever He opens the door.

One day an idea struck—to go back to the prototype: "How did Jesus and His disciples evangelize others?" I was sure there would be copious books on the subject, but when I began to research, I was surprised to find very little written about how Jesus interacted with non-believers. I examined New Testament encounters Jesus and His disciples had with different kinds of people. I noticed when Jesus dealt with religious people, He was often sarcastic and even upset with them for not being kind and loving toward others. I also noticed when Jesus was around unreligious people, He often demonstrated God's power by performing a miracle or speaking a prophetic word to them. He would then tell them more about the Kingdom of God.

After researching every encounter Jesus had with unbelievers, I realized Jesus and His disciples never used the verses we use for evangelism. The evangelism recorded in the New Testament is not the evangelism we practice today! In addition, the United States, which was founded upon religious freedom, is no longer the nation upholding Christian values some consider it to be. Many Christians have become more secular in their thinking. Often those we are targeting for evangelism do not believe in the Bible's validity. Since many evangelistic methods employ Bible verses, this makes our evangelistic methods in need of updating all the more.

We Are All Missionaries

At some point it dawned on me that if our evangelistic methods aren't working in society and the world is growing more and more secular, then we need to approach evangelism as if we were foreign missionaries. We wouldn't show up in a new country and assume its citizens would respond to "Just be born again!" Instead we would study the culture and language of those we are attempting to reach and begin to establish relationship so we could effectively communicate Jesus' message.

Some missionaries to North American Indian tribes are having great success using Bill Bright's *Four Spiritual Laws* pamphlet. In this case, this older evangelistic method works because it fits the North American Indian culture, where many tribes believe four spirits hold the universe together. So, to them, the concept of the *Four Spiritual Laws* is intriguing.[5]

Churches in the United States have always sent missionaries abroad. In recent years, I have met missionaries who have been sent from other countries to reach people in the United States. However, it is a testimony providing a dramatic wake-up call for those who have ears to hear of just how radically our society is changing. I began to pray and ask God to show me how I could learn to be a missionary right where I live. I started studying about missionaries, and some had wild stories of how God used them to reach people. One day a friend told me about Don Richardson's first book, *The Peace Child*, which documents his experience among the Sawi, a tribe of cannibals in New Guinea. After futile attempts to "explain" Jesus to the Sawis, Richardson finally found a means to communicate the Gospel message through an important Sawi cultural belief: When the Sawi were warring with another tribe, the two tribes would each exchange one of their tribal chief's sons to ensure lasting peace. This act engendered a treaty that would not be broken, for if a tribe started to fight again, their chief's son would immediately be killed. Armed with this cultural metaphor, Richardson was able to explain that Jesus was God's peace child to them. It worked.

In his second book, *Eternity in Their Hearts*, Richardson explains that God has placed events and prophecies within an unreached society's history and culture to prepare them in advance for future missionaries who will come and explain their meaning. In 1776, he recounts hundreds of native tribespeople in the jungles of Burma being greeted by a white-skinned stranger in hope that he would be the one to bring "the book" their forefathers had lost so many centuries before. The book had told the secrets of Y'Wa, the supreme God. Later missionaries were astounded at how God had prepared these people for one of the greatest mass conversions in history![6]

Stories like these confirmed what I was seeing happen at Streams Dream Teams and revelatory outreach events. God is speaking to people all the time through circumstances and life events, waiting for us to encounter people and tell them more about what God is saying to them.

The Missing Ingredient

Richardson emphasized that the key to reaching people cross-culturally lies in the encounter Saul of Tarsus had with Jesus on the Damascus road. Saul recognized Jesus as Lord and was soon called to be a missionary to the non-Jewish peoples (Acts 9).

What Jesus said to Saul was particularly important:[7]

> As he [Saul] neared Damascus on his journey, suddenly a light from heaven flashed around him. He fell to the ground and heard a voice say to him, "Saul, Saul, why do you persecute me?" "Who are you, Lord?" Saul asked. "I am Jesus, whom you are persecuting," he replied. "Now get up and go into the city, and you will be told what you must do." The men traveling with Saul stood there speechless; they heard the sound but did not see anyone. Saul got up from the ground, but when he opened his eyes he could see nothing. So they led him by the hand into Damascus. For three days he was blind, and did not eat or drink anything.
> —Acts 9:3–9

Saul, later renamed Paul, a man who had once persecuted and put Christians to death, went on to become an apostle who took Jesus' message throughout Europe and Asia, and started many churches as a result of his encounter with Jesus. His writings make up a good portion of the New Testament. Saul explains more of what happened on the road to Damascus when he recounts his experience to King Agrippa (Acts 26).

Jesus said to Saul:

> "I will rescue you from your own people and from the Gentiles. I am sending you to them to open their eyes and turn them from darkness to light, and from the power of Satan to God, so that they may receive forgiveness of sins and a place among those who are sanctified by faith in me."
> —Acts 26:17–18

Jesus told Paul that he would "open [people's] eyes" and "turn them from darkness to light." I had always been taught we are to help turn people from darkness to light, and from the power of Satan to God, but I never remembered hearing about the need first to open people's eyes. This revelation confirmed what I had always felt: Coming to Jesus

Christ is a process! First our eyes are opened, and then we can turn from darkness to light.

This key was the missing ingredient in reaching people for Jesus. However, it seemed to conflict with what I had been taught about evangelism—to share Jesus with as many people as possible and to ask if they wanted to receive Jesus Christ into their hearts. Whenever I did this, I never considered where such individuals might be in their process and journey with God.

After Saul (Paul) encountered Jesus, he was blind and was led by hand to the city of Damascus. A Christian named Ananias responded to a vision from God and sought Saul out, placing his hands on Saul's eyes, and then God brought healing (Acts 9:10–20). Even Saul had to have his eyes opened, and that happened through a miracle, which brought him physically and spiritually from darkness into light. Immediately he began to evangelize others, sharing that Jesus was God's Son. If Jesus instructed Saul to open people's eyes so they could turn from darkness to light, and since we as disciples have Jesus as our model, let's begin with this approach.

How Did Jesus Do Evangelism?

An hour before I was to lead a workshop on evangelism, I was sitting in a hotel room and immediately turned to the book of John to look for encounters Jesus had with nonreligious people. God began to show me how Jesus reached people. What I found was the following:

Jesus Encounters Nathanael (John 1:45–51)

Jesus drew Nathanael to follow him by giving him a word of knowledge. It must have been accurate because Nathanael was amazed that Jesus knew him. Jesus also told Nathanael that earlier he had been sitting under a fig tree; perhaps it was where Nathanael had his prayer times with God, a place he could retreat to and let his hair down—for didn't Jesus call Nathanael a man of truth? Jesus went on to give him a word of prophecy for the future. This encounter opened Nathanael's eyes and caused him to believe in Jesus and become one of His followers.

Jesus Encounters People at a Wedding Reception (John 2:1–11)
This was Jesus' first recorded miracle, and what an astounding and symbolic one at that! Jesus knew the people needed a savior but He also knew they had not had enough time with Him to understand the details of this. Jesus met the people's needs by providing new wine, which also gained His disciples' attention because when they saw the miracle, they put their faith in Him. This miracle would make a great outreach in bars!

Jesus Encounters Nicodemus, a Religious Leader (John 3:1–21)
This is a powerful example of being a missionary and learning to communicate with people in their "language." Jesus demonstrates this in His encounter with Nicodemus, a rabbi and teacher of Jewish law.

Nicodemus came secretly to Jesus seeking more information about His message. At first glance, it's easy to miss the depth of Jesus' response to Nicodemus. In "missionary terminology," Jesus honed in on an aspect of Nicodemus' belief system by which He could relate His message: the Jewish culture and mind-set of that time. Unlike the Western way of thinking, Jews viewed life on earth as a gestation period or prenatal experience in a womb, before birth into the true life of Paradise or Heaven. Life for a Jew encompassed the eternal reality of the spiritual world. In the Western world, life is considered as space and time on earth, and Heaven is at a time in the future.[8] Through the lens of the more holistic Jewish mind-set, we can more fully appreciate the brilliance of John 3:3: "I tell you the truth, no one can see the kingdom of God unless he is born again." Jesus went on to reveal more to Nicodemus, although at the time Nicodemus had trouble believing (verse 12).

The encounter with Nicodemus is one of the few in Scripture where Jesus sat and reasoned with someone without demonstrating God's power. Jesus knew that Nicodemus was an intelligent man versed in the Scriptures, so Jesus did not take the approach of refuting and quoting Scriptures to him. Instead He translated His message into Nicodemus' cultural understanding and hinted that the signs concerning Himself were the fulfillment of biblical prophesies.

It obviously worked because Nicodemus later became a believer, standing up for Jesus during a meeting (John 7:50) and helping to bury Jesus' body after His crucifixion (John 19:39).

Jesus Encounters the Samaritan Woman (John 4:7–30, 39–41)

Interestingly, in this encounter the Samaritan woman was aware that Rachel met Jacob, the man who changed her life, at a well (Genesis 29:10). Yet, little did she know she was about to meet a man at Jacob's Well who would also change her life. During their conversation, Jesus told the Samaritan woman a little about herself: she had been married five times and was not married to the man she now lived with. He did this without condemning her; He did it by a word of knowledge. As a result, the woman's response was "Sir, I perceive you to be a prophet." Nowadays, most people's response to this kind of clear insight would be "Are you a psychic?"

Jesus had appraised her accurately: she was a relational nightmare. His compassion and concern for her, however, seemed to cut through her doubts, igniting such an evangelistic flame in her that she ran back to the town to tell everyone about Him and causing many Samaritans to seek Jesus that day. Later those who before this encounter would probably not have interacted with her at all told her: "We no longer believe just because of what you said; now we have heard for ourselves, and we know that this man really is the Savior of the world" (John 4:42). They, too, had had their eyes opened, and God turned them from darkness to light.

Jesus Encounters a Roman Official (John 4:46–52)

Jesus left Samaria and healed the son of a Roman noble without even meeting the child or laying hands on him. This miracle transcended distance, and the father realized his son had been healed at the exact moment Jesus declared "Your son will live." So the Roman noble and his entire household believed in Jesus (John 4:53).

Jesus Encounters a Paralyzed Man (John 5:1–9)

Jesus healed a man who had been paralyzed for thirty-eight years. Not only was the man healed but he also required no rehabilitation after not using his legs for decades. After performing a miracle Jesus was able to give him further spiritual counsel:

> Later Jesus found him at the temple and said to him, "See, you are well again. Stop sinning or something worse may happen to you." The man went away and told the Jews that it was Jesus who had made him well.
> —John 5:14–15

Jesus Encounters Five Thousand Hungry People (John 6:1–13)
Jesus and the disciples fed five thousand people miraculously by multiplying five loaves of bread and two small fish. This was an eye-opening extravaganza en masse! It must have worked because John 6:14 records:

> After the people saw the miraculous sign that Jesus did, they began to say, "Surely this is the Prophet who is to come into the world."

Jesus Encounters His Disciples on the Water (John 6:16–21)
Jesus walked on the water and caught up with his disciples in the middle of the Sea of Galilee. It's easy to miss—amid details as to how far Jesus' disciples had rowed before they saw Him walking on the water—just how significant this encounter with Jesus really was. Then when Jesus got in the boat, He, the boat, and twelve of His disciples were immediately and miraculously transported by the Spirit to the other side of the Sea of Galilee. This was so amazing that it caused an immediate increase in the disciples' faith.

Similar to this encounter was what happened to Philip after he baptized the Ethiopian eunuch. The Spirit of the Lord took him away, and he appeared at Azotus (Acts 8:39–40).

Opening People's Eyes
Throughout the first six chapters of the book of John, Jesus employed various means to "open people's eyes" before preaching to them. He demonstrated God's love and power in practical ways, with each

encounter tailor-made to touch the particular individual or group He was addressing. Jesus used the spiritual gifts of words of knowledge and wisdom, prophecy, healing, and miracles. Yet, He did not neglect to respond to their material, physical, and emotional needs as well—feeding the hungry, loving the outcasts, and bringing truth even when it caused Him to be hated. In short, whatever would get people to recognize the power and love of God, He did. As a result, people were looking for Him at the Feast of Tabernacles:

> Now at the Feast the Jews were watching for him and asking, "Where is that man?"
> —John 7:11

This set the stage for Jesus to get up publicly at the Feast of Tabernacles and boldly proclaim:

> "Whoever believes in me, as the Scripture has said, streams of living water will flow from within him."
> —John 7:38

If we faithfully follow Jesus' model, seeking to do the Father's will more than our own, we will be led to opportunities to open people's eyes and draw them to God, and they will actually seek us out and be open to talking about God.

A pastor friend of mine took up my challenge to survey the New Testament accounts of Jesus' interactions with unbelievers. My friend observed that more than anything else, Jesus healed people. So if we are to practice Jesus' pattern, shouldn't we focus on healing? My response to my friend was that Jesus lived at a time when the greatest need was for physical healing. People were plagued with leprosy and many other debilitating conditions and even a simple illness could result in death. Today we do not have that same kind of desperate need for healing. Though nowadays our need for physical healing may not be as acute; we still need it as well as emotional, relational, and spiritual healing. The good news is that we can touch others today in the same way that Jesus did during His time on earth.

CHAPTER

5

HOW CAN WE DO IT?

J esus promised that we would perform "greater works" than He did (John 14:12) and that in so doing, we will make disciples of all nations. We must believe God wants to touch others by His Holy Spirit through us. In speaking at numerous churches across the United States, I've ascertained that many Christians believe God still gives spiritual gifts and uses people in these gifts. However, many do not see their gifts being used very often, and others do not even know which spiritual gifts they possess.

When I first became a Christian, I was surprised to find that believers do not agree on what they believe. I expected all I had to do was believe Jesus died for my sins and go to church, and I'd be set. But I soon found out there were more choices for me to make, and I had to discover and decide what to believe. This is the nature of theology.

One of my first church experiences was with a group who called themselves "conservative evangelicals." Theology was very important to them, but, I later learned, their theology often limited God's power and left no room for miracles. This group basically believed the Holy Spirit's gifts, such as healing, miracles, and prophecy (1 Corinthians 12, Ephesians 4, Romans 12), had been to launch the early Church, and died with the first apostles. Theologians referred to this as the "cessa-tion theory" of the Holy Spirit's gifts.

Frankly, I found this idea hard to accept, since I had already person-ally experienced God's power, gifts, and healing in my life. Would the God who poured out His power and gifts on Christians for a century suddenly say: "Y'all have the Bible now, and you're pretty intelligent. You don't really need my gifts and power any more."

Since God has given us specific promises about the gifts in His Word, how could this be true?

> "In the last days," God says,
> "I will pour out my Spirit on all people.
> Your sons and daughters will prophesy,
> your young men will see visions,
> your old men will dream dreams.
> Even on my servants, both men and women,
> I will pour out my Spirit in those days,
> and they will prophesy.
> I will show wonders in the heaven above
> and signs on the earth below,
> blood and fire and billows of smoke."
> —Acts 2:17–19

God does not change, and He gave, gives, and will continue giving men and women His gifts and pouring out His power on His people. It is not by our own might or power, rather only by His Spirit that we can accomplish these greater works Jesus foretold . . . and we need them to enlighten the hearts of a lost, dying world.

Healed of Huntington's Disease

In 2001 I was diagnosed with a rare, incurable genetic malady called Huntington's disease, from which five family members had already died, including my mother. As early symptoms set in, I had to leave my job as a pastor. My life and ministry seemed near an end; needless to say, I accosted God to get healed.

In the midst of my despair, some good friends took me to a meeting of Brother Albert Ramirez of Faith International Prophetic Ministries in Campbell, California. Brother Albert has an accurate prophetic gift and believes in healing. Without knowing anything about my situation, Brother Albert called me forward to pray for me. He declared God would heal me, and I would evangelize in a novel way. He also added that in a short period of time, I would be traveling around the country training people.

I desperately wanted to believe this prophetic word from God, so I began to attend healing meetings every chance I could. A few months later, I felt something ripple out of my body while revivalist Todd Bentley prayed for me. I believe God healed me of Huntington's disease despite DNA tests still coming up positive. My symptoms are gone, and I feel great. Furthermore, less than a year after I was healed, I joined the staff of John Paul Jackson's Streams Ministries and began traveling around the country training people in prophetic evangelism—a blatant fulfillment of God's earlier prophetic word to me through Brother Albert. Thus I cannot believe spiritual gifts have ceased, since I am a living testimony of God's healing virtue and miracle-working power to propel us into our destinies.

Blessed with Spiritual Gifts

To practice evangelism à la Jesus, we must have faith to believe God still gives His people spiritual gifts through the Holy Spirit. We must also ruthlessly tear down any hindrances to those gifts operating in us. God still does everything recorded in the Bible. Implore Him to pour out more and more of His Holy Spirit into you every day. Don't settle for less than a banqueting table; instead be a lover who will ravish the Bridegroom's heart. We need God's Spirit fresh and new in us every day.

> Don't be deceived, my dear brothers. Every good and perfect gift is from above, coming down from the Father of the heavenly lights, who does not change like shifting shadows.
> —James 1:16–17

We should welcome God's use of us to bless others. The Holy Spirit abides in all believers, and we all have access to the Spirit's gifts according to His desires. As we take risks and grow in our spiritual gifts, God will use us to draw people to Himself.

> The body is a unit, though it is made up of many parts; and though all its parts are many, they form one body. So it is with Christ. For we were all baptized by one Spirit into one body—whether Jews or Greeks, slave or free—and we were all given the one Spirit to drink.
> —1 Corinthians 12:12–13

Ultimately, to evangelize as Jesus did, we need to be in close relationship with those who need God's love. As we develop friendships with people outside the Church, we will quickly discover that people respond to us best when we are being real and transparent. This means we must avoid acting or sounding religious around secular people.

When Jesus told Peter to fish in deep waters, He also told him he would catch people not just fish (Luke 5). By providing a meaningful example, Jesus illustrated the reflection between natural and spiritual dimensions. Just as Peter had caught fish, he would catch people for Jesus. He was actually saying to Peter, "I am going to use you just as you are—a fisherman." Similarly, Jesus wants to take each of us just as we are—with the personalities we have, in the jobs we already hold, in the churches we belong to—and use us to advance His Kingdom.

We cannot catch fish in shallow water. Shallow water depicts our safe comfort zones, like staying within the ship of our friends and familiar elements. Jesus must be at the helm if we are to catch fish. We must have an intimate relationship with Him in order to influence others. The fish are in deep water. Fishing in deep water may represent communing with acquaintances or coworkers who are secular and getting to know and going places with them without our religious shtick.

Ways of Sharing God's Love
As we seek to understand how we can influence people with God's love, we need to understand the various styles of evangelism. Different methods of evangelism reach different kinds of people. The following list has been compiled from my own experience, as well as from various writers and sermons I've heard over the years.

Confrontational Style: This is one of the most popular styles and is the stereotypical evangelistic method. It involves handing out evangelistic tracts, street preaching, sign waving: TODAY'S THE DAY OF SALVATION! This style might be successful if the people are open to Christianity and God has been drawing them along in the process; however, if people are not open to Christianity, they will put up a big wall if you use this style, and you won't be able to talk with them.

Invitational Style: Most people feel comfortable with this style. Philip went and got his friend Nathanael, and without spending lots of time explaining the Messianic Scriptures, he stated, "Come and see."

I have a friend who is a master of the invitational style of evangelism. He invited more people to church than anyone I knew, and if not for his invitation, many might not have had the opportunity to come to Jesus.

Service/Servant Style: People with the gift of hospitality naturally flow in this style, which involves displaying God's love through acts of kindness. Often this style melts the hearts of unbelievers by demonstrating God's unconditional love. Some people may go into nursing homes, while others may stand on street corners giving out free sodas. Servant evangelists help cultivate an atmosphere where unbelievers feel more comfortable letting down their "walls" because they feel loved and cared for. In the Scripture, Tabitha was a woman who filled her days with acts of kindness and charity (Acts 9:36). Mother Teresa once said, "Small things done with great love can change the world."

Intellectual Style: This evangelistic style appeals through logic and reasoning to analytical, curious people who love to play "hard ball" by asking difficult questions. It reaches people who like a systematic, cerebral approach. Paul used this style when he reasoned with the Jews in the synagogue, with the Gentile worshippers, and with the philosophers in the Athenian marketplace (Acts 17:16-32). C. S. Lewis used this style throughout his writings and discussions in the academic world.

Testimonial Style: Everyone whom God has touched has a story to tell of what He has done in his or her life. People love to hear how God shows His power in our lives. It's like the story of the blind man who was healed by Jesus. The formerly blind man couldn't explain to the Pharisees about the Messiah, except to offer a testimony: "One thing I do know. I was blind but now I see!" (John 9:25). People are more likely to listen to a testimony than to a sermon. Hearing that God is transforming lives and situations today gives them hope that God can help them with their own problems.

Friendship/Relational Style: This is probably the most popular evangelistic style among everyday people. It involves making friends with people, spending time with them, praying for them, and waiting for God to open doors of opportunity to share more about who He is and what He means to you. The friendship style of evangelism worked powerfully in the 1980s and '90s. It still works today, except that people are so busy they rarely have time to cultivate friendships. Levi (Matthew) was a tax collector who invited his coworkers to a party to meet Jesus (Luke 5:29).

Power/Prophetic Style: Power evangelism became popular in the 1980s when John Wimber used spiritual gifts, healing, miracles, and revelation from God to draw people to Jesus. It was Jesus' *modus operandi* to demonstrate God's power to someone and then explain it. He used the word of knowledge, the word of wisdom, and prophecy to cause people to reflect about their lives. Approaching people with positive feedback from the Holy Spirit will get their attention and it may open the door to further discussion about Jesus and the supernatural.

All of these evangelistic styles can be useful, depending on the people and situations involved. I encourage you to discover your natural evangelistic style and to begin operating in it. If you have the spiritual gift of hospitality, invite people over for a party! Or if you enjoy acting as a host outside the home, invite people to a worship service, event, or retreat. Find the evangelistic style that best suits your personality, because when you are yourself, people are more likely to listen and receive what you have to say.

Steve Sjogren puts it into a modern-day parable:

I liken sharing the good news to playing golf. The rules of the game allow thirteen different clubs to be carried in the golf bag—each one appropriate at some point in the game. . . .Imagine a golfer going out with only a putter. . . .We need an entire "golf bag" of approaches for reaching people in our communities.[1]

Understanding the Process

If we want to help people come to know and understand God's love, we must perceive where they are in their spiritual journey toward God, which involves a process of circumstances and events. Each person's journey is unique. Some people have to go through many difficulties before they surrender their lives to Jesus; others do not. Sometimes it's hard to assess where non-Christians are in this process of surrendering control of their lives to God, but it is essential to discern this before you can appropriately engage them. With sincere intentions, some Christians may ask non-Christians if they would like to receive Jesus as their personal Savior without knowing whether such individuals even understand who Jesus is or what a "personal Savior" actually means.

Evangelism is much like planting and harvesting seeds. Jesus often explained God's Kingdom with the analogy of planting and harvesting. The apostle Paul said, "I planted the seed, Apollos watered it, but God made it grow" (1 Corinthians 3:6). Jesus concurred:

This is what the kingdom of God is like. A man scatters seed on the ground. Night and day, whether he sleeps or gets up, the seed sprouts and grows, though he does not know how. All by itself the soil produces grain—first the stalk, then the head, then the full kernel in the head. As soon as the grain is ripe, he puts the sickle to it, because the harvest has come.

—Mark 4:26–29

Notice the process a seed of grain undergoes to reach maturity. First it is scattered, then it sprouts. Over time it grows, producing a stalk, then a head, then the full kernel, before finally it is ready to be harvested. We would never plant a seed and then immediately try to harvest it. It must pass through a cycle of growth.

Likewise, we would never pick a rosebud and expect it instantly to burst into bloom. It must open on its own, in its own timing. Yet this is exactly what we are doing when we try to force people to pray "the sinner's prayer" before they really understand and are ready. Evangelism is a process. Realizing that we must treat each person differently is necessary in ensuring people receive the wonderful message of Jesus.

Process evangelism is:

1. Realizing people tend to come to Christ over a period of time and through a process of circumstances and events.
2. Trusting that God will water any seeds we plant.
3. Being low-key and looking for divine opportunities to talk about God in a nonreligious, nonconfrontational way.
4. Developing relationships with non-Christians by hanging out with them, praying for them, and waiting for God to open doors of opportunity.
5. Respecting people for where they are in their spiritual journey and inviting them to share their views on God without us trying to correct their theology.
6. Understanding that God will use your efforts to help *nudge* people closer to a relationship with Him.

Process evangelism is not:

1. Feeling we must immediately "close the deal" and "sell" Jesus to someone in order to succeed at evangelism.
2. Being confrontational in a rude way (1 Peter 3:15).
3. Quoting Bible verses to a person who does not accept the validity of the Bible.
4. Being driven by our need to perform for God.

Discerning Where People Are

Often I shock people in my evangelism training workshops when I tell them our goal for the event is *not* to lead people to Jesus Christ today! Our goal is simply to discern where people are in their process and to help nudge them a step closer to Jesus.

Not everyone we will encounter today is ready to be led to Jesus. If we go out with the goal of leading people in the sinner's prayer, we might communicate too forcefully, try to rush the process, and end up alienating them.

The best material I've ever come across on process evangelism is by James Engel, who researched and understood people's decision-making process. His findings could be applied to consumers and businesses, besides those on a journey to Jesus Christ. He developed the Engel Scale, a spiritual decision-making process scale introduced in his book *What's Gone Wrong with the Harvest.*[2]

John Wimber and Peter Wagner created a Modified Engel Scale, which was published in Wimber's book *Power Evangelism* in 1985.[3] This scale distinguishes various levels spiritual seekers tend to experience on their journey to Jesus. It also shows the evangelist's role in helping seekers reach each level.

I have taken the Wimber/Wagner version and modified it slightly to focus on the steps someone would take who is in the process of coming into a relationship with God. This includes a series of steps before and after people reach salvation. Salvation is just the demarcation point of starting a new life; afterward, much work is still needed to help guide people toward spiritual maturity.

God has a unique "eye-opening" approach for each person. Once someone's eyes are opened, he or she will be able to understand God's love for him or her.

My version of the Modified Engel Scale is called Process Evangelism: The Revised Addison/Engel Scale. I hope it will help you better understand the decision-making process people follow and what we can do to help them.

In evangelism outreaches, after pinpointing where we believe people are in their decision-making process toward Jesus, it is important to gear our conversation and language to each person's particular level.

Then I have found individuals often are very open to talking about spirituality and their needs.

Negotiating this process may feel a bit awkward at first and may seem like "watering down" or compromising the Gospel message. But this concern will disappear as a depth of conversation develops with someone in need and his or her walls of resistance go down. When we see process evangelism actually working, then we want to master the process.

After venturing out with one of the Streams Dream Teams and having interpreted the dream of a young man who was tattooed and pierced, one pastor found himself in an intense conversation with the young man. Using nonreligious language, the pastor met the young man at his level, prompting him to pour out his heart to the pastor. The young man was significantly touched. He was also nudged a step closer in understanding God's love. Later the pastor excused himself and found a quiet place where he wept, realizing his original ministry calling was to reach people like this young man.

PROCESS EVANGELISM

Many more post-conversion steps needed for spiritual maturity

SALVATION   ↑   NEW DISCIPLE IS BORN

Our Role				Seeker's Condition
Be a Friend and Be Available	Demonstrate God's Love and Power	Explain Practically	Persuade	1 Asking forgiveness of sin and having faith in God.
				2 Challenge and decision to act.
				3 Awareness of his or her need for God.
				4 Positive attitude toward Christianity.
				5 Grasps the cost to be a Christian.
				6 Awareness of the basic facts of Christianity.
				7 Interest in Christianity.
				8 Initial awareness of Christianity.
				9 No effective knowledge of Christianity.
				10 Awareness of spirituality.
				11 No belief or interest in spirituality.

SPIRITUAL DECISION PROCESS

Be a friend and be available: Pray for the person, genuinely care for him or her, and wait on God to open opportunities to spend time with him or her.

Demonstrate God's love and power: Use spiritual gifts to demonstrate God's love, power, and encouragement.

Explain practically: Explain the message of Jesus using one of many tools such as *The Bridge, The Romans Road to Salvation, Steps to Peace with God*, etc., or by using modern parables from movies. Share your own experience with Christianity.

Persuade: Since God has been already drawing this person and he or she understands Christianity, you can ask the person if he or she wants to commit their life to Christ. Then talk about what that means. Ask the person to pray and invite Jesus into his or her life.

Adapted from *What's Gone Wrong With the Harvest* by James Engel and Wilbert Norton (Grand Rapids: Zondervan, 1975), p. 45.

Explanation of the Revised Addison/Engel Scale

You can nudge people closer to a new life in Jesus by using the revised Addison/Engel Scale. Once you determine where people are on the scale, you can communicate and relate to them at the level where they are. Thus, you stand a better chance of their responding positively to you, and God will use your actions to help draw them a step closer to Him.

Let's start at the bottom of the scale.

Level 11: No belief or interest in spirituality—A person who is not interested in God or religion. *[Note: The first three points apply to every level of the scale and will not be repeated in subsequent points.]*

1. Be a friend, and be available for people, as God directs. Let your life be a witness to them, but don't push your views. Pray for them, genuinely show interest, and wait for God to open opportunities to spend time with them.
2. Use spiritual gifts to demonstrate God's love, power, and encouragement.
3. Talk at a deeper level, being sensitive to God's leading. If conversa-

tion occurs, thoughtfully listen to them, and they will listen to you.

4. Limit how far you go with conversations, unless God leads you further.
5. Don't take rejection personally.

Level 10: Awareness of spirituality—A person who might believe in God but whose views of God may vary. He or she is often open to all gods.
[1, 2, and 3]

4. He/she is usually much more open to talking about spirituality and the supernatural.

Level 9: No effective knowledge of Christianity—A person who is open to God and to Jesus but who may view Him as a teacher or prophet.
[1, 2, and 3]

4. He or she may ask questions, but be careful to avoid overwhelming him/her, because he/she probably doesn't understand as much as you may think.

Level 8: Initial awareness of Christianity—A person who may have grown up around church or had Christian family members. He or she has basic knowledge but lacks understanding. He or she may never have had a spiritual awakening or may have been hurt by a Christian or by a previous church experience.
[1, 2, and 3]

4. He/she probably won't ask many questions because he/she feels as if he/she knows all or should know more about Christianity. Often he/she is very opinionated or may feel shame.
5. Many of his/her views may be skewed by a bad experience or past hurt.

Level 7: Interest in Christianity—God has already been working in this person's life. He/she may have grown up going to church, but usually without any bad experience.
[1, 2, and 3]

4. Often God will speak to him/her in a dream, or through a circumstance or a crisis, and he/she will come to you or come to church to find out more.

5. It's usually your relationship and concern for him/her that will build the bridge to understanding God's love for him/her.

Level 6: Awareness of the basic facts of Christianity—This person may have had contact with other Christians. He/she grew up in church or had a Christian family member. Or perhaps he/she had a spiritual awakening and fell away during the process to maturity. This person is often willing to come to church or to Bible studies.
[1, 2, and 3]
4. Because his/her contact with Christianity may not have been positive, he/she may be open to talking, but proceed carefully with love and patience.
5. It's usually your relationship and concern for him/her that will build the bridge to understanding God's love for him/her.

Level 5: Grasp the cost to be a Christian—This person is beginning to understand that following Jesus comes with a cost: a commitment of time, energy, and resources.
[1, 2, and 3]
4. This is a crucial juncture where people are often pressured too soon.
5. Explain the message of Jesus to him/her using one of many tools— the Bridge, Romans Road, etc.—or by using modern parables from movies.
6. Share your own experience with Christianity.
7. You may be tempted to dilute the message to get him/her to commit. In the long run, it will be better if you tell him/her the cost involved.
8. Give him/her time to seriously think about what you have shared, and follow up.
9. Don't be alarmed if he/she says no.

Level 4: Positive attitude toward Christianity—This person is beginning to be attracted to Christianity. Or he/she grew up in a Christian home and is returning to his/her faith.
[1, 2, and 3]
4. He/she is open to going to church and to Bible studies.
5. He/she is eager to learn but not ready to receive Jesus Christ as

his/her Savior.

6. Explain the message of Jesus to this person using one of many tools—the Bridge, Romans Road, etc.—or by using modern parables from movies.

7. Share your own experience with Christianity.

Level 3: Awareness of his/her need for God—God has been drawing this person through crises or circumstances. This person has definite needs that must be met.
[1, 2, and 3]

4. He/she is usually "ripe" and ready because God has gotten his/her attention.

5. Do not assume this person knows how to pray or what to do next.

6. Explain the message of Jesus to him/her using one of many tools—the Bridge, Romans Road, etc.—or by using modern parables from movies.

7. Share your own experience with Christianity.

Level 2: Challenge and decision to act—The message of Jesus is understood, and a decision needs to be made to turn over the control of this person's life to Jesus. This must be done with sincere intentions and not just from head knowledge or feeling pressured to "pray the prayer." The Holy Spirit is drawing this person.
[1, 2, and 3]

4. Ask if he/she wants to commit his/her life to Christ, and talk about what that means.

5. Ask the person to pray. (It does not need to be a word-for-word rehearsed sinner's prayer.) Or offer to pray with him/her. Some individuals may want to go home and pray alone, and this is okay, too.

Level 1: Asking forgiveness of sin and having faith in God—This person turns over the control of his/her life to Jesus Christ.
[1, 2, and 3]

4. His/her life is regenerated in the Spirit.

5. This is the beginning of a new life in Christ.

Salvation: New spiritual life—"Ground Zero."
1. You must follow up with this person and talk more about his/her decision.
2. Demonic forces may discourage him/her, hinting that what he/she did was meaningless or misguided.
3. A sincere commitment must have been made in order for him/her to resist Satan's temptations.

There are many more steps to becoming a disciple of Jesus. Salvation is just the beginning. The person will need to commit to a church, make new Christian friends, get baptized, receive the fullness of the Holy Spirit, discover and use his/her spiritual gifts, find a place to serve, and give his/her time, energy, and resources to God.

By understanding the revised Addison/Engel Scale, we can work with the Holy Spirit and help draw people closer to Jesus. Here is a typical encounter I had on one of our recent outreaches that illustrates this process in a real-life situation. Two women were interested in having a dream interpreted. The woman with the dream seemed very open when I unfolded its meaning. The dream referred to turmoil in her life, and she agreed that the interpretation was accurate.

At this point, I really didn't know where these women were on the process scale. I needed to ask some fact-finding questions and proceed as long as they kept the walls down. So I said to the dreamer, "Dreams are very spiritual. You seem like a spiritual person. Are you?" It was a way of asking if she was a Christian or not. Most people will tell you outright. The woman with the dream replied, "Yes, I am a very spiritual person."

Since she did not have any walls up, I took the conversation to the next level. I asked the Holy Spirit about her and her friend, and I repeated to the dreamer what I heard. "You do something with your hands and it brings healing to people." She smiled and said she was a New Age massage therapist.

At this point in the conversation, I knew she was at least at a Level 10 (had an awareness of the supernatural). Using discernment from the Holy Spirit, I sensed that she might have grown up in a home where her parents occasionally went to church. So I assumed she was probably at a Level 8 or 9 (had an initial awareness of Christianity, or she had no effective knowledge of Christianity). At these lower levels, it is safest to be friendly and demonstrate God's love in a practical way.

Then I looked at her friend and conveyed what I was hearing from God about her. "There is something important about the color pink." Both the woman and her friend burst into laughter because she had just painted her bedroom pink, and she hates pink. I was impressed by the Holy Spirit that pink was her mother's favorite color, and that the woman's artistic talent came from her mother. She looked at me with tears in her eyes and nodded yes.

Turning my attention back to the first woman, I heard the Holy Spirit tell me to ask her about her spirit guides. When I did, she leaned toward me and quietly said, "I am so glad you asked. I think one of them might be bad for me."

This encounter went on for several minutes, and any walls they had erected were lowered. Since God had given me such accurate revelation about them, I wanted them to know where this revelation was coming from. I revealed that I was a Christian and not a psychic, but I was not like any Christian that they had ever met. Surprised, they replied, "We never knew Christians could hear God like that." At this point, they were open and ready for anything. So I bumped them to Level 7 (interest in Christianity). If they believed that Christians could hear God this accurately, then they were definitely interested.

I began to wonder if these women might actually be at a Level 6 (awareness of the basic facts of Christianity). So I went on to tell them about new light that was coming into their lives. One replied, "I have been asking for new light." I briefly told the first woman that her traditional, religious upbringing would soon make more sense. Then I began to sense a hesitation in her. So I stopped.

I had taken the encounter as far as I could without damaging what God had already done. Both she and her friend were amazed that a Christian could tell them about their lives with such accuracy and kindness. Now it was up to the Holy Spirit to send someone else to follow up and bring both women closer to Him. The women gave me their first names, and I pray for them regularly.

In other encounters when I ask people if they are spiritual, they might tell me they went to church as a child but have not been there in a while. This would put them at a Level 6 (awareness of the basic facts of Christianity). Most likely they would not be open to us sharing the Gospel with them at this point.

We want to make sure that people are between Levels 5 through 1 before we share the facts of Christianity with them. Then we can talk about God and how God has touched our lives. If you want to stay in close relationship with people, you will need to be very sensitive to where they are.

God can orchestrate an encounter demonstrating His power and love that will stir people to ascend several levels closer in one conversation. When we understand that evangelism is a process, we will not feel pressured to induce someone to "pray the prayer." We don't need to use only the old standard ways, like handing out tracts or Bibles; we can also explore new and creative ways to share God's love such as our gifts, dreams, the arts, movies, or media to explain more about Jesus.

Sometimes we meet people who already are noticing God at work in their lives, as the following story depicts. One of our Streams Dream Team members, Jolene, was at work for an Internet retail company, and the computers went down. She had some free time, so she decided to walk around the office. The Holy Spirit drew her to a coworker whom she did not know very well. As she and the woman talked, Jolene sensed the Holy Spirit advising her that the woman had a true gift of compassion. As Jolene conveyed this to the woman, she also explained that this was a gift from God and that it really touched people. Encouraged, the woman beamed with hope. She told Jolene she was thinking about going back to church.

Jolene began to converse with the woman about her spiritual needs. She was open and wanting more. Before the computers came back up, the woman happily prayed a prayer of salvation right in her cubicle. This happened easily and quickly because God had already been preparing her and drawing her to Him.

Jolene used the gift of a word of knowledge to cause the woman to open up and become interested in talking. Jolene recognized that the woman went from a Level 3—awareness of her need for God, to a Level 1—asking forgiveness of her sin and having faith in God. Nudging people one step closer to Jesus is just as important as helping them take the step to salvation.

Communicating Without Sounding Religious

In writing this book, I spent a great deal of time studying nearly every book about evangelism available. For two years I did on-the-street laboratory research by leading outreach events in various cities around the United States and United Kingdom, and I have concluded that many Christians need a reawakening to the actual message and methodology of Jesus, in order to reach people outside the Church. We really need to take a serious look at how we share the love of God with non-Christians. One of the biggest barriers to sharing God's love with outsiders seems to be our communication style. The apostle Paul was also very concerned with how he communicated with outsiders and gave a warning to the early Christians about it as well:

> ...pray for us... that I may proclaim it clearly, as I should. Be wise in the way you act toward outsiders; make the most of every opportunity. Let your speech always be full of grace, seasoned with salt, so that you may know how to answer everyone.
> —Colossians 4:2–6

As I mentioned earlier, I had at one time been involved in the New Age movement, but after having a radical encounter with Jesus in 1985 and later finding a caring and helpful Christian church, I began to receive emotional and spiritual healing that allowed me to grow and mature in my new Christian life. I consider myself one of the lucky ones who was able to stick with the process of becoming a part of the Christian community. I say this because many other people I knew with similar experiences left the Christian community because they were turned off by Christians and by the Church.

After being involved with a Christian church for a number of years, I realized I had cut myself off from relationship with my non-Christian friends. These were the people who needed God the most. I also noticed that I had developed a "church vocabulary," and I was using religious words outsiders did not understand. I wanted to bring Jesus' wonderful, life-changing message to the lost but lacked the ability to communicate it in language they could understand.

Our society has changed dramatically over the past few decades.

Although we live in a country with many churches and purported adherents to Christian values, for most people a Christian heritage is no longer passed down from the previous generation. A plethora of broken relationships, divided families, and alienation abounds; people need God.

Perhaps that is why God led me on a journey that helped me reconnect with people outside the Church. For a number of years I volunteered at a homeless mission and visited inmates on death row. By simply spending time with the outcasts of society, I came to realize how much God loves people. I found that if I talked to people without using religious language, they were very interested in hearing more about God. In the process I was able to develop relationships with many people outside the Church.

When I tried to converse with someone who had no religious background, in words and phrases that were religious lingo, I might as well have been speaking in tongues to him or her. The apostle Paul addresses this issue in 1 Corinthians 14:9–11:

...Unless you speak intelligible words with your tongue, how will anyone know what you are saying? You will just be speaking into the air. Undoubtedly there are all sorts of languages in the world, yet none of them is without meaning. If then I do not grasp the meaning of what someone is saying, I am a foreigner to the speaker, and he is a foreigner to me.

Although Paul was addressing the issue of speaking in tongues, we, too, are like foreigners when we speak to non-Christians in "insider" religious language. Paul was very strategic in communicating with those outside the church. In evangelistic outreaches, people are very open to talking about God, if we use language they can understand.

I have also found a great number of people who don't have a relationship with Jesus or don't go to church because they have been turned off by Christianity. Perhaps this occurred from having a negative experience with an over-zealous religious family member, or from having been wounded by a legalistic Christian. These individuals are familiar with Christian lingo, but they can be put off by religious sounding words. For them, hearing

Christian lingo is like getting salt rubbed into their wounds.

Much "Christianese" can be attributed to the fact that modern Bible translations have been available and popular for only a few decades. The well-known King James Version (KJV) translates the Greek and Hebrew of the Bible very beautifully, but it was written in a style that was archaic even at the time of its publication but that was chosen because it was both dignified and impressive. The King James translation is very useful for word studies, but it does not flow well in today's conversational English. We have all memorized Scripture verses and then found ourselves repeating them verbatim in our conversations. This influences how we speak when we transition into an evangelistic mode. The King James has a beautiful poetic flair, but many words and phrases sound stilted or are unintelligible in current, everyday conversation. Some King James words and phrases which have crept into Christian parlance are: "like unto," "likened to," "whereby," "saith the Lord," or "thee," "thou," and "ye," and all the "iths," "eths," and "ests" added as suffixes. I admonish thee: It behoovest ye ill to utter thusly whilst thou sojournest at the coffeepot at work!

In his book, *Evangelism That Works*, George Barna notes that many popular Christian tracts have wording that is hard for people who do not have a religious background to understand.[4] Some phrases George Barna found in popular tracts and hymns, and a few of my own, are listed at the end of the chapter. Next to each I have added my suggestions on ways to convey the same message in nonreligious language. It's hard to believe some of these phrases are still in use today, but to me old habits of our Church culture are hard to break, especially if they are not perceived as a problem.

I pastored a church in a college town with a sizable New Age and Wiccan population. Many visited our congregation, and I realized rather quickly that I needed to speak their language if I wanted to reach them. For the first few months I asked my leaders to write down every religious word I spoke into the microphone. We brainstormed better ways to convey ideas effectively, and it helped me become conscious of the importance of clear communication.

A few practical steps in learning to talk to people without sounding religious are:

1. List religious words Christians use regularly. Notice how often you say them, and explore new ways to convey the same message. This list might include words like: *blessing, anointing, praise, amen, sanctified, glorify, call of God, mantle, covering, bondage, open heaven, favor*, etc. There's nothing wrong with using these words in Christian settings, though.

2. Try reading a modern translation of the Bible such as the *New Living Translation, The Message*, or *The Good News Bible*. Look up verses you know, and note how differently they are worded from the way you may have memorized them.

3. Use a thesaurus, and find good substitutes for religious words. You may have to use more words to capture your intended meaning; for instance, "call of God on your life" can be translated as "You have a higher purpose in life. You are a person who wants to make a difference in people's lives."

4. Pursue relationships with people outside your Christian circle. Whenever you have the chance, go to a party with coworkers, invite a neighbor to coffee, or go to lunch with a non-Christian. Just be friends without feeling as though you have to lead everyone to Jesus. Remember, the Holy Spirit is the One who convicts people of their sin, not us. Jesus merely called us to love people.

We can learn to be sensitive to people who may not know much about the Bible. God may give us a prophetic word of encouragement for someone, and we can learn the skill of communicating it so it is clearly construed and palatable to receive. I have a booklet, *No More Christianese: Replacing Religious Language with Everyday Words* available through my website **www.dougaddison.com**.

Here is a list of Christianese colloquialisms, along with some non-religious alternatives:

Anointing: You have special characteristics. People seem to be drawn to you.

Authority: You are a very take-charge kind of person. You have clout. You are able to easily influence others. You are about to gain greater control of some situations in your life.

Be fed by the Word: We receive spiritual insight from reading the Bible.

Blessing: Good things; something good is coming your way; benefits; advantages.

Bondage: Trapped, restrained.

Born again: Spiritual awakening, spiritual experience.

Burden: Concern for; solicitous of _____; care for _____.

Call on your life/Call of God: You have an appointment with destiny. You have a greater purpose in life.

Calling: What you were created to do. You are uniquely gifted to _____.

Cleansing: Refining, purifying, healing; some things need to be changed; giving up some old habits.

Covered with the blood or washed in the blood: Your sins have been forgiven because of Jesus' dying on the cross.

Do not trust in yourself: Learn to trust God more than your own feelings.

Faith: Trust what you cannot see yet. You feel like there is more to life.

Favor: Good things are coming your way; God is smiling on you.

Gifts or giftings: You have special ability to _____. There's something special in your personality.

Grace: Things are going to be easier. Someone is going to cut you some slack.

Healing: Things are going to change for the better. You are recovering from _____.

Holiness: Doing things right; getting it together; staying pure.

Judgment: Trouble.

Mantle: Something you have been created to do. You have a special purpose in life to _____. You are naturally gifted to _____. You may have always felt that there is more to your life _____.

Ministry: Something you have been chosen to do, a destiny; an assignment from God (said humorously).

Open heaven: Your mind is going to get much clearer. Answers are going to come to some questions you've had. Things will start going your way. Things will start coming together for you.

Perseverance: Sticking with it even when things are hard.

Possess a broken spirit or a contrite heart: You need to be humble, open, and willing to learn.

Prophetic: Able to see and understand spiritual things. Visionary.

Prophecy: Insight.

Praise: Thankfulness. Happiness. Appreciation. Gratitude.

Prayer: Reflection. Meditation. Contemplation.

Purity: Doing what is right. Staying away from things that may be bad for you.

Pursue the Christian walk: Become a Christian; find out more about the message of Jesus.

Reap what you have sown: Some things you have done may come back on you; there is a price to pay; what goes around comes around.

Road to righteousness: The spiritual journey to God.

Redemption: Change for the good; salvage what has been lost.

Repent of thy transgressions: Ask God's forgiveness for what you've done wrong.

Resurrect/Resurrection: Come back to life. Big-time change. New life. Metamorphosis. Transformation.

Revelation: New insight. Get clarity on a situation. Some questions will be answered for you. Gut feeling(s).

Sanctify your soul: You need to grow and mature spiritually. There is a higher justice. Now is a time to look at, or deal with, your issues.

Satan/demons: Something negatively influencing your life. Negative forces.

Saved by grace: We get a new spiritual life that is not based on what we do—it's just because God loves us.

Season: Period of time.

Seek fellowship with the Holy Spirit: Allow the Holy Spirit to personally guide you, or get a close relationship with God through God's Holy Spirit.

Spiritual covering: Mentored by someone who can help guide you. Get in community.

Spiritual food: Information that is going to be helpful.

Spiritual gifts: Special characteristics. Uniqueness. You make a difference.

Stronghold: Something holding you back. Obstacle; hindrance. In a rut.

Strongman: Something opposing you or holding you back; spiritual resistance.

Vision: (okay to use in some contexts) Clarity. Seeing things in a different light. Getting some questions answered. Getting perspective. Change of perception.

Wilderness: A time when things are not very clear. Difficult times. Hard times. The pits.

Wisdom: Good advice. Knowing the right thing to do. Smart counsel.

Words that are okay to use: destiny, energy, Creator, God (use instead of Lord, because Lord suggests a condition of your heart where you have progressed along the scale to where you call Him Lord), insight, light, meditate (often the New Age word for prayer), spirit, spiritual, vibe, vision.

New Age words to avoid: Reincarnation, astral projection or astral travel, channeling, mantra.

PUTTING *a* PROPHETIC SPIN *on* EVANGELISM

CHAPTER

6

WE'RE NOT
ALL PROPHETS—
UNDERSTANDING
REVELATORY GIFTS

T he words *prophetic* and *evangelism* are scary to many Christians, especially when used in the same sentence. The words *prophetic* and *prophecy* connote myriad misconceptions, stereotypes, or bad experiences. Pastors often ask me not to use the word *prophetic* in their churches. Nonetheless whatever the experience has been, these words are in the Bible and directly correlate to spreading the good news. Revelation 19:10 states: "For the testimony of Jesus is the spirit of prophecy." Just because some people have had bad experiences with the prophetic does not condemn it's integrity, or mean it's inherently bad.

As a pastor I've seen the gift of prophecy help people change and endure hard times. I've also seen this gift misused by immature people lacking character and instruction in this gift's appropriate use. Since we have not understood and valued revelatory gifts from God, the teaching and pastoring of their appropriate use has been limited and frequently neglected.

No gift from God is born mature; every gift needs instruction and mentoring in its use. I often hear people remark, "God gave me this gift, so why do I need to be taught? It's from God, right?" If God gifted your pastor to guide people, wouldn't he or she still need to be trained? Or to put it in a more secular arena, Mikhail Baryshnikov might have been born with an innate talent for dance, but if he hadn't undergone decades of rigorous ballet instruction to harness the natural gift, we probably would not know his name. When God gifts teachers to instruct, they first need to study before they can teach. When God gifts an evangelist or missionary, they still need to prepare before ministering to others. When it comes to the prophetic gift, it is no different. Unfortunately, until recently there has been little parenting or training about revelatory gifts.

Another issue with prophecy is that people possessing this gift, or thinking they possess it, too often view themselves as prophets. Being a prophet requires consistently operating with a high level of accuracy, character, and favor and usually involves decades of preparation, training, and commissioning from God. Whenever people brandish a title and thereby expect people to listen to them, they run the risk of becoming "entitled." People are not compelled to listen to us even though we may be speaking God's very words unless we have gained favor and credibility with them. We gain favor gradually by being actively involved in healthy relationships in a local church.

Unfortunately many prophetically gifted people have suffered rejection because they've not known how to use their gifts appropriately. Rejection often drives a person to isolation, and so many prophetically gifted people end up roaming from church to church. Eventually some fall into believing they are lone prophets and that people have hardened their hearts to God's voice.

The reality may be that the prophetically gifted person's own character flaws prevent people from listening to him or her. It's a vicious cycle that often occurs in the life of one gifted to hear God's voice. There's hope, however; proper training and love can restore these gifted outcasts to the Church. One of the most practical messages I've ever heard on how to pastor prophetic people and be pastored in the prophetic is John Paul Jackson's *Developing Your Prophetic Gift* (available from Streams Ministries International.

The gift of prophecy can offer wonderful experiences to help us hear from God. Yet Christians need to put spiritual gifts into their proper perspective. Spiritual gifts, including revelatory gifts, function in a church just as it needs greeters, Sunday school teachers, and a worship team.

In 1999 my wife and I were pastoring a church in the Midwest. God had called us to start a church that would reach spiritual outcasts, and for us then this meant people in the New Age movement. It was not an easy time for us. I worked a second job to make ends meet, and that year seven people died in my family, including my mother. So, we were pretty worn out and broken as we drove to a conference one Saturday evening where John Paul Jackson was speaking. I had never met him, but I had benefited from his teaching over the years. I was so beaten down and disillusioned that before entering the conference, in fact, I told my wife, "Maybe starting this church was a mistake. It's too hard on our family. Let's just close it down and go back home to California." John Paul began closing the session by choosing people in the audience to stand while he prophesied over them. After delivering encouraging words from God to several people, he turned in our direction and asked my wife and me to stand. He told us many things about ourselves that were accurate, then declared, "Young man, the vision God gave you to reach into a realm of outcasts is real, and it will bear fruit." That was all we needed to go on. We didn't close the church; it still exists today.

We had desperately needed encouragement. We had needed to hear God speak into our situation. The gift of prophecy, when used properly, will expel darkness in people's lives and guide them into their proper destiny. The key is learning to use our revelatory gifts properly. One of the misuses of prophecy is to point out a person's sin. An even worse misuse of the gift would be to publicly point out the sin. People don't need to have their sins pointed out to them; they already know their sins. It's much more beneficial to encourage them with what God has planned for them once they've gotten through their sin.

At one point when I was going through a deeper level of inner healing and facing the temptation of old behavior, John Paul Jackson looked at me in that inimitable way of his, expressing divine compassion, and although he could have told me everything I was doing wrong, he simply said, "Doug, you can take all the promises God has made to you and multiply them by one hundred, once you deal with these issues in your life." His word gave me the encouraging boost I needed to persevere and pursue a higher level of spiritual maturity.

Sharing Jesus' Message

We are all called to evangelize, but we are not all called as evangelists. Likewise, we all have the ability to operate in the gift of prophecy, but we are certainly not all prophets. Sometimes I can hear God clearly, but I do not consider myself a prophet. The gifts of the Spirit are available to all of us, but few of us are called to the office of either evangelist or prophet.

Prophecy is simply a form of revelation from God. Revelation is communication from God. Most Christians agree that God speaks in various ways. He can speak to us through the Bible or by song lyrics, from a picture, an impression in our minds, or with a "sense" or intuition. God can speak to us through a dream or vision, or even through an audible voice. The ways God speaks are unlimited, because God is limitless. Only our own beliefs or perceptions of God limit the way He speaks to us. Despite this, God can surpass our wildest imaginations in how He chooses to speak with us (1 Corinthians 2:9).

If you have ever shared the message of salvation, then you have experienced the gift of prophecy. As mentioned earlier, "For the testimony of Jesus is the spirit of prophecy," which an angel told the apostle John in Revelation 19:10. When we share the wonderful message of Jesus, we are doing it through the gifts of the Holy Spirit:

> "But you will receive power when the Holy Spirit comes on you;
> and you will be my witnesses in Jerusalem, and in all Judea and
> Samaria, and to the ends of the earth."
> —Acts 1:8

We must convey God's love not *just* with our words but with God's power through the Holy Spirit. Convincing people to pray the sinner's prayer when they do not believe it in their hearts will not accomplish their salvation if performed without unction, and may ultimately turn them off to God more than if you'd left them alone. The Bible states that we require the Holy Spirit's intervention for a person to respond to our message. Therefore, people will only respond to our sharing about Jesus if the Holy Spirit has already been drawing them. Jesus Himself said, "This is why I told you that no one can come to me unless the Father has enabled him" (John 6:65).

We cannot proclaim, "Jesus is Lord" and really mean it in our hearts without the Holy Spirit's revelation (1 Corinthians 12:3). When Peter attested that Jesus was the Son of the living God, Jesus apprised Peter it could not have been revealed to him by man, but only by God (Matthew 16:16–17).

How does this all tie in with evangelism? As I explained in the chapter on process evangelism, there are many ways to share God's love. Jesus and His disciples used spiritual gifts through the Holy Spirit. They listened to God, and, as Jesus said in John 5:19, He could only do what He saw the Father doing.

God is often already at work in a person's life, and we often need only piggyback on His work. By using our ability to hear God, we can ask Him to point out those people who are already partway along in the process. Who is it that needs to be encouraged today? This allows us to zero in on people in our everyday lives without having to stand on street corners asking hundreds of people if they want to know more about Jesus.

What Is Prophetic Evangelism?

Prophetic evangelism is using any form of divine revelation that brings people closer to a personal relationship with Jesus Christ. It may be in the form of a dream interpretation, a word of knowledge, or a word of prophecy. Knowing whom to approach with the Gospel message is also an important function of our revelatory gifts. We want to engage those God already has in process, so when we "do" prophetic evangelism, we should be just as concerned with whom to talk to as with what to say.

As I discussed in Chapter 4, Jesus employed prophetic evangelism when he sought the Samaritan woman at the well (John 4:15–20). He engaged her in a conversation and then sparked her attention by discussing water—water one drinks once, which then embodies an eternal need. Once He'd secured her attention, He immediately switched to a word of knowledge about her five husbands. The woman said to the townspeople: "Come, see a man who told me everything I ever did. Could this be the Christ?" Many of the Samaritans from that town believed in Him because of the woman testifying: "He told me everything I ever did" (John 4:28–30, 39).

Interestingly, the woman was asking Jesus to give her what He had—living water. I've discovered that when we make contact with the people God is drawing to Himself and give them a revelatory word, they often respond like the Samaritan woman—they ask us to give them what we have. This evangelistic approach is quite different from those where we ask people if they want what we have. People will believe in our God when we can "tell them everything they ever did."

I took a Streams Dream Team to Manchester, England, for the 2002 Commonwealth Games. One of our groups was dining at a pub and decided to put a FREE SPIRITUAL READINGS sign up at their table to test the waters. A woman walked by a few times, then sat down at our table and blurted, "I want to be spiritually cleansed!" She next described a dream she'd had showing situations and relationships in her life that needed to be handled. The team members at the table began telling the woman how much God loved her, and she lit up with hope. When they went on to explain that God could heal her emotions and relationships, she asked: "How can I get this?" As the team members prayed with her, she actually experienced the Holy Spirit's presence. Warmth suffused her entire body, as well as relief, as if weights had dropped off her. Often when people encounter God, they will beg you to give them what you have! It's not unusual for them to acknowledge, "I haven't dreamt in ten years, but last night I had a dream" or to confirm "I've been thinking all day about the very thing you just said to me."

Now Is the Time for Prophetic Evangelism

I personally believe that prophetic evangelism is one of the most effective styles of evangelism to reach people today. Many people consider themselves spiritual, though they may not identify with "Christianity" because they were disappointed or hurt by an earlier religious experience. Prophetic evangelism opens the door to touch people where they are and demonstrate God's love by affirming them with information we would never know without divine revelation.

Every day we come in contact with hordes of people who are unaware that God loves them (or for some, that there even is a God). Too often our efforts to reach them actually further turn them off to God. Imagine the possibilities if we could convey the love God's heart bears for them. What an impact it would make! The face of someone who's just had an encouraging word delivered from God that shatters hopelessness and despair is one of the most splendid and spiritually satisfying sights to behold.

One day I was witnessing to a woman, mentioning how much God cares for her, when I interjected, "Do you mind if I tell you what I think God is saying about you right now?" Eagerly she welcomed the prospect. I briefly closed my eyes and immediately saw a rose. I informed her that God sees her as a rose, commenting on how lovely roses are and how they brighten up the day. Her eyes grew large and she remarked, "I just saw some roses this morning, and I thought to myself how pretty they were. All day I've been noticing roses everywhere!" This little encounter got her attention. The picture of a rose was a word of knowledge. I would not have seen it unless God showed it to me. The word of knowledge gift is a very effective tool to reach people, and it makes evangelism fun.

The most common fear people have about the word of knowledge is "What if I'm wrong?" Well, if I'm wrong, I try again. I tell the person I'm interacting with that I'm practicing learning to hear God. Practicing means I'm not perfect; it takes me off the hook.

What actually happens if we are wrong? There will be times when we miss it, especially during the training process. As long as we are focusing on encouraging people, we will still have a positive effect on them. We just try again. The more we practice, the better we will be able to hear God.

Sometimes people will tell us what we said didn't relate to them, while in reality, it actually touched them so deeply it frightened them and they pretended we'd missed it. I just laugh this off and chalk it up as "strike one." This kind of evangelism grows easier as you practice on more people, and eventually it becomes possible to speak regularly and deeply into people's lives.

We'll learn more about how God speaks to us and how we can hear His voice for others in the next chapter.

In his book, *Prophetic Evangelism*, Anglican pastor Mark Stibbe recorded this encounter he had at Heathrow Airport:

I arrived at Heathrow around eight o'clock in the morning, having prayed that in the next twenty-four hours while traveling to New Mexico I would have divine appointments with seekers. What I didn't anticipate was how quickly this prayer would be answered!

At Heathrow I headed to the check-in desks. I was being ushered to the first class check-in (even though I wasn't traveling first-class) when I saw a closer check-in counter become available and felt drawn there instead, where a young woman in an airline uniform waited to serve me. She appeared to be a Muslim or a Hindu, in her early thirties.

As I approached the desk and noticed her eyes, two words came to mind: sadness and rejection. The eyes are the windows of the soul. They are often such a giveaway. I reached the desk and greeted, "Hi, how are you today?" Even though I was chirpy and polite, she wouldn't reply. So I carried on just giving my details. After a few minutes I decided to try again. "Are you sure you're okay?" At this her eyes started to well up. "You're suffering from rejection, aren't you?" I continued. At this she opened up and started to tell me how her boyfriend was rejecting her and how people had rejected her all her life. "Everyone in my life has rejected me," she concluded. "God hasn't," I replied. "In fact, He's a perfect Father, and He's crazy about you."

I tried to console her. I gave her a copy of my book *The Big Picture* (coauthored with J. John) and instructed her to look at the chapter called "In Search of the Father." She then asked whether I lived nearby, and I said yes and gave her the details of my church. Next she asked if she could see me and how much it would cost! I told her that she could come and visit, and it would be free. She gave me her e-mail address, I gave her mine, and then she shook my hand, looking so much brighter![1]

A Sign

When I first began studying prophetic evangelism in the Bible, I was drawn to the apostle Paul's statement that prophecy is a sign to believers, not unbelievers. I've received a good deal of e-mail from Christians insisting that I shouldn't use the gift of prophecy for unbelievers because of 1 Corinthians 14:22, "Tongues, then, are a sign, not for believers but for unbelievers; prophecy, however, is for believers, not for unbelievers."

At first glance it sounds as if Paul is saying we shouldn't use prophecy for unbelievers. But if you read this verse in context, you will find that two verses later he states that prophecy will help the unbeliever to fall down and worship God.

> But if an unbeliever or someone who does not understand comes in while everybody is prophesying, he will be convinced by all that he is a sinner and will be judged by all, and the secrets of his heart will be laid bare. So he will fall down and worship God, exclaiming, "God is really among you!"
> —1 Corinthians 14:24–25

Jesus also used prophecy with unbelievers (John 4). The key to understanding 1 Corinthians 14:22 is the word *sign*. A sign indicates that God is present. It is the proof that God is with you. Paul is explaining that if you use the gift of tongues, referring in this case, I believe to the type of tongues—that is, actual known languages—mentioned in Acts 2, then unbelievers are more likely to know God is with you because you are supernaturally speaking their language.

Christians seem to have lost the art of reading the Bible in context! We can't take a verse out of context to prove a point. Throughout this book I've quoted many verses to provide a biblical grounding on prophetic evangelism. The points I've sketched are recurring themes throughout Scripture. None of them contradict Jesus, as 1 Corinthians 14:22 does if taken out of context.

CHAPTER
7

HEARING GOD

L earning to hear the voice of God is a lifelong process. It is so simple that many children actively hear God regularly. Jesus said in Mark 10:15 that we must receive the Kingdom of God as a little child would, and keeping a childlike mind-set will certainly help us to hear God better. If one were to ask children how God speaks, they would probably reply, "I don't know. He just does it." Children don't get hung up on how or why; they focus on the limitless possibilities of a God who is a loving heavenly Father.

God still speaks to His children today; He never stopped speaking to us. Yet we seem to have lost track of how He speaks or we limit how He speaks by our beliefs. Most Christians can hear God through an application of what they read in the Bible or when praying for someone; they may testify of feeling led by God to do something (marry someone, take a particular job, buy a particular car, etc.). These are some of the most common ways people hear God's voice.

God speaks to us through His Holy Spirit. We use the spiritual gifts to hear and interact with God and others. These gifts are mentioned several times in the New Testament. The most familiar references are 1 Corinthians 12, Ephesians 4, and Romans 12. The apostle Paul encouraged us to understand our spiritual gifts and not be ignorant of them.

> To one there is given through the Spirit the message [word] of wisdom, to another the message [word] of knowledge by means of the same Spirit, to another faith by the same Spirit, to another gifts of healing by that one Spirit, to another miraculous powers, to another prophecy, to another distinguishing between spirits, to another speaking in different kinds of tongues, and to still another the interpretation of tongues. All these are the work of one and the same Spirit, and he gives them to each one, just as he determines.
> —1 Corinthians 12:8–11

The revelatory gifts mentioned in First Corinthians are: word of wisdom, word of knowledge, and prophecy. Ephesians 4:11–12 mentions five ministry/office gifts: apostle, prophet, evangelist, pastor, and teacher. The gifts mentioned in First Corinthians appear to be general gifts all of us can operate in. The five ministries mentioned in Ephesians 4 are usually viewed as actual positions people have as they mature and operate in spiritual gifts at higher levels. Thus we can all prophesy, but we may not all be prophets. We can all evangelize, but we are not all going to be evangelists.

Here's an explanation of the three revelatory gifts mentioned above:

- **Word of knowledge:** Something you would not have known about a person or situation unless God had told you. It usually concerns the past or the present.

- **Word of wisdom:** Wisdom that comes from God, not wisdom of this world. Often it is a divine solution or advice that when applied will bring lasting change. This gift often allows you to see beneath the surface and pinpoint root issues of problems.

- **Prophecy:** A message from God about a past, present, or future situation.

Hearing God through the written Word is not mentioned as a gift in the Bible, but we see this happening in the New Testament (Luke 24:27–34; Acts 8:34–37).

In the same way, dreams are not listed among the gifts either, although they are mentioned in Acts 2 when Peter quotes Joel's prophecy describing the last days. Since we witness God speaking to people in their dreams throughout the Bible, we know this is one of the ways He chooses to communicate with us.[1]

There are many misconceptions about how revelatory gifts should be used in churches. Paul declares, "But everyone who prophesies speaks to men for their strengthening, encouragement and comfort" (1 Corinthians 14:3). All prophecy or revelation from God, whether a word of knowledge, a prophetic word, or a dream, is intended to build people up, not to pronounce judgment on them. Notice that the words correction and judgment are not mentioned.

The Old Testament is rife with examples of prophets being sent to Israel proclaiming God's judgment if people didn't repent, but this was before Jesus Christ's coming and thereby, the Holy Spirit's personal empowerment to everyone who believes and receives Him. I would encourage prophetic individuals to stay within the New Testament guidelines of 1 Corinthians 14:3.

As we grow in spiritual maturity, our character becomes of much greater value to God than our spiritual gifts. We can easily get out of balance by putting too much emphasis on spiritual gifts and prophetic words and fail to grow in what matters most to God—the evidence of a changed life. When we get to Heaven, we will be judged *not* on how great our spiritual gifts were on earth but rather on our character (2 Corinthians 5:10). Character is who we are when no one is looking. Character is the Holy Spirit's fruit evidenced in our lives.

But the fruit of the Spirit is love, joy, peace, patience, kindness, goodness, faithfulness, gentleness and self-control.
—Galatians 5:22–23

As I persist in dealing with my own character issues, God allows me greater influence with others. I may continue to hear God the same as always, but as my character increases more people will listen to what

God communicates through me. As a result more people will be changed through revelatory words from God.

The subject of learning to hear God could fill many books. I am only giving a brief overview and touching on the highlights of how to hear God for yourself and others.

Everything I mention here, I do regularly or have experienced sometime in my life. Here are some practical steps in learning to hear God consistently.

1. Believe that God wants to speak to you.

For God does speak—now one way, now another—though man may not perceive it.
—Job 33:14

Most Christians believe that God speaks to people, just not to them. And if we continually focus on not being able to do something, chances are we never will. But if we change our focus and accept that God loves us and longs to speak to us, there is a good chance we will begin to hear God in ways we never thought possible. This is not positive thinking; it is a spiritual principle of how unbelief chokes out supernatural experiences from God (Matthew 13:58).

God desires to commune with us. Most of the time we simply need to clear away some of the busyness in our lives to perceive Him. He longs to convey messages to us through our dreams and visions (Job 33:15–16), through the Bible (Daniel 9:2), through a conversation we've have with someone (wisdom), and through the arts (music, dance, paintings, sculpture). The possibilities are endless.

Sometimes our own theology can block our communications from God. Looking back, I realize God had spoken to me on many occasions, but I did not recognize His voice until I began focusing on hearing Him. Often I only realized it was God speaking to me much later, while at the time of occurrence I simply wrote things off as coincidences or chance experiences.

Once I was convinced God actually wanted to communicate with me and guide me on everyday issues, I was eager to spend time with

Him. God longs for us to spend time with Him. Sometimes He gives us a puzzling dream just so we will search out the answer. And when we find the answer, it might seem insignificant but God loves us so much that He is thrilled when we search for Him as we would for buried treasure. We can often miss God's still, gentle voice if we do not slow down enough to listen.

2. Make sure you are at peace and have intentional times of quiet.

But Jesus often withdrew to lonely places and prayed.
—Luke 5:16

To hear God, it's so important to have peace in your life. As my friend John Paul Jackson says, "Peace is the potting soil for revelation." When we are hurried or stressed out, we are least likely to consistently hear God.

Many people hear God when they are in the shower. This may seem surprising, but it's because it's one of the few places where we are alone and able to listen.

It's good to set time aside regularly—daily, if possible—to quiet yourself. For me the best time is first thing in the morning. I know we are all wired differently, but morning seems to be a good time for me because the phone isn't ringing yet and things are the quietest. After a good night's sleep, we are more spiritually alert. God often speaks in a still, small voice in our mind that can be subtle and easy to miss if we don't take time to listen.

Each morning I try to spend a minimum of fifteen minutes "centered" or focused on God. I usually spend another forty-five minutes praying, reading the Bible, and asking God to speak to me about my day.

For me it's best to combine my prayer time with exercise so that my body, soul, and spirit are all working together. I take a brisk walk, do stretches, or just get out and move around. When my life gets too hectic, I usually have ignored taking time to listen to God. Consequently I end up getting less done than if I had spent an hour or more focusing on God first.

There was a time in my life when no matter how much I had to do and how hard I worked, I always seemed to end the day feeling overwhelmed. So I did an experiment. For a week I spent two or three hours every morning walking, praying, reading the Bible, listening to an inspiring tape, and prayerfully planning out my day. I discovered that I got more done and felt more fulfilled at the end of each day than if I had worked a grueling twelve-hour day. I was even able to end my work just in time to have dinner with my family.

Since that time I have made it a priority to set aside at least an hour a day to hear God and get centered on Him. My whole day flows; I tend to have fewer "fires to fight," and I get more accomplished. If you are not taking time to get centered on God and hear Him each day, then I challenge you to make a plan right now to do just that. Fifteen minutes is all it takes. Start small, and slowly increase your time alone with God.

I cannot overemphasize the importance of reading your Bible regularly. The more we know God's Word, the easier it will be to recognize His voice. We must know God's ways, His character, and His nature, which are found in the Bible. As we learn more of who God is, then we will be able to discern whether we are hearing from God, our soul, or demonic sources.

God will often speak to us by impressing a verse on our minds. Reading the Bible daily will help condition us to be more spiritually sensitive. A friend was going to court for a minor legal matter, and that morning he quieted his heart by reading the Bible. He felt impressed by God to read Psalm 37. Verse 33 stood out to him: "...but the LORD will not leave them in their power or let them be condemned when brought to trial." Later as he entered the courtroom, he discovered the minor issue had turned into a major matter. He did not have an attorney, and although he was not at fault, it could potentially cost him thousands of dollars. Because God had directed him to Psalm 37:33, he prayed and left himself in God's hands. When his case came up, the judge ruled in his favor.

Sometimes God speaks to us clearly, as in the court case. At other times He is not as clear. "It is the glory of God to conceal a matter; to search out a matter is the glory of kings" (Proverbs 25:2). God often conceals matters and requires those who really want more of Him to search for God as they would to uncover hidden treasure. If we spend time with Him, we will access the treasures of kings!

3. Respond to what God says to you.

But the one who hears my words and does not put them into practice is like a man who built a house on the ground without a foundation.
—Luke 6:49a

As God begins to speak to you, it's a good idea to value these words and write them down. Get a notebook, a prayer journal, or type them in your computer—whatever fits your personality and style. Then get into the habit of writing down what you sense God telling you. This will help you keep track of them. Give thanks to God when you see them happening, because it helps your spirit to focus positively on God's good nature.

If we want to hear God consistently, we must be quick and faithful to respond every time He speaks. Sometimes God will remain silent until we do the last thing He told us to do. Stop for a minute and ask God to show you whether there is anything you need to respond to. God sometimes wakes me up in the middle of the night and speaks to me. Then I noticed this stopped happening, so I asked God to show me whether anything in my life was hindering my spiritual growth.

Shortly after that I woke up at three o'clock in the morning and felt God demand, "Get up! I want to speak to you." I dragged myself to the living room and waited. I didn't hear anything, so I turned on the television. On one of those middle-of-the-night infomercials, God spoke to me about how I handle my time and my need for exercise. Once I applied what He revealed that night, my life changed radically. Later I realized He had already shown me this twice before in the past year. I had rejected it because it came in the form of an infomercial. Since I responded to this message I again frequently hear God at night.

4. Remove hindrances to hearing God.

Therefore, since we are surrounded by such a great cloud of witnesses, let us throw off everything that hinders . . .
—Hebrews 12:1

On your journey to hear God, we will run into hindrances. One of the biggest hindrances is unbelief. Unbelief immediately derails our ability to hear God. Jesus Himself could not perform miracles in Nazareth because of the people's unbelief (Matthew 13:58). Believe in God's limitless power, for "with God all things are possible" (Matthew 19:26).

Another hindrance to hearing God is our own theology. If we were taught that God does not speak today, then this will affect our ability to hear Him. Our traditions or forms of worship can also be a hindrance to hearing God because they often limit when God can speak.

When I first began to grow in my ability to hear God, I had to be in a worship service to hear Him. I really don't know why, but I believed that if God was going to speak to me, it would probably be at church. The drawback to my way of thinking was that the church I went to at the time had a quick, seeker-friendly service that did not allow much time to be quiet and listen to God.

At times I would hear God clearly through a word of knowledge or a prophetic word, and I would go to the pastor and share it. He believed it was a word from God, but the traditions of the church I was attending would not allow us to share prophetic words at a Sunday morning service. Most prophetically gifted people would probably have been offended and would have gone off to join a new church, claiming that the pastor was grieving the Holy Spirit. I stuck with it, stayed at the church, and believed that if God was really speaking, then He would make a way to touch people.

This same church had an early-morning prayer meeting each week; one morning I had a word of knowledge that someone was about to have a heart attack. We prayed for the person, and then I went off to work. Later that morning I received a call from the church office informing me that one of the elders present at the prayer meeting had had a heart attack. He was thought to have a ruptured aorta. One of the doctors at the hospital was also an elder at the church and had been present at the prayer meeting that morning. She reminded him that God had spoken about his condition that morning and that we had already prayed for him. By the time doctors got him in to examine him, he was completely healed and they sent him home.

Needless to say, when someone has a major heart attack on

Thursday and is in church feeling fine the following Sunday morning, it is a huge miracle! The story and the word of knowledge were shared at the service, and God got the glory! Although the traditions of this church didn't allow a prophetic word in the Sunday morning service, God gave me a prophetic word at an early-morning prayer meeting that allowed us to pray for a man's life. God got the glory for the man's healing, and everyone in the main church service heard about it.

A third hindrance to hearing God is being too busy to listen. Sometimes we can fill our time with activities that appear worthwhile but actually hinder us from spending time hearing God. These activities can take the form of Christian books, tapes, radio programs, or TV, which are not necessarily bad for us, but if we substitute them for spending time with God, they can become hindrances. If this is the case for you, a solution might be to watch one less television program and instead commune with God.

A fourth hindrance to hearing God is to assume we know what He is saying. This is called *presumption*. Often God speaks to us to reveal barriers and blocks in our relationship with Him. Our own ego and pride can block the real meaning of what God is trying to show us. We may think He is speaking about something or someone else and not about our own issues.

One man approached a church leader with a dream he'd had. The dream indicated that the dreamer was operating out of his own strength, and not out of God's gifts through the Holy Spirit. However, the man claimed that God had told him the dream was for the leader and not for him (the leader was not even in the dream). As a result, not only did he miss the change God wanted to accomplish in his life, but it also caused hurt feelings and mistrust from the leader. It's always best to be humble and teachable and not assume anything.

Hearing God in Daily Life

Wouldn't it be great to hear God tell you to take a different way to work, and as you did, you avoided a huge accident on the freeway? Or to hear God subtly nudge you to buy flowers for your spouse, and when you got home you found your spouse had one of the worst days ever? How about hearing God tell you to go to the bank and remove a certain amount of money, and later that day you were in need of that exact amount of cash?

These are ways God wants to interact with us regularly; however, to hear God consistently and accurately takes practice.

> But solid food is for the mature, who by constant use have trained themselves to distinguish good from evil.
> —Hebrews 5:14

One reason many Christians do not hear God consistently is because they have not practiced listening. They may also have trouble discerning whether what they hear is from God, themselves, or other sources. Practice is required to grow and mature in our spiritual life.

To get a job at a bank's Fraud and Security Department, you need to be able to distinguish between real and counterfeit money. To be able to distinguish between the two, you would need some real money and also some counterfeit money for comparison. Once you sensitized yourself to the differences, you could then tell whether or not other money is real just by touch or looks, because you have become sensitive through practice. These same principles apply to hearing God. We must learn to be sensitive to the differences between God's voice, our own ideas, and those of demonic forces.

I was working as a business information services manager (MIS) several years ago. While I was driving up the freeway after work, I was celebrating and thinking about what my next career move should be, because I had just completed a five-year career goal. "God, show me my next goals," I requested. The Holy Spirit whispered to me, "Turn on the radio." I immediately turned on the radio and found a Christian radio station that was broadcasting a message from Dr. Charles Stanley, who was exhorting in his Georgia accent: "Now you listen here. Jesus is your goal." God used that experience to guide me to my next career move—full-time ministry.

Once you have heard God accurately a few times, you will begin to recognize how His voice comes to you, the tone, the sense, the taste, and smell (so to speak). And when you have also heard what you thought was God but lacking the same attributes and characteristics, you will eventually be able to differentiate between the genuine and the counterfeit. You can often tell a counterfeit word because it will not line up with the Bible. A true revelatory word from God never violates biblical principles.

One morning before work I was having a quiet time, and I sensed God counsel me to wear a tie that day. As a computer consultant I usually dressed corporate casual. But that day when I arrived at work, I was unexpectedly asked to meet my boss at the office of a client who was an affluent man in the entertainment industry. As I entered the client's office, I noticed my boss was also wearing a tie, and he was surprised to see me wearing one, too. I would have never done that without spending time to hear God each day.

So, how can we practice hearing God? Ask God to begin to train you. Ask the Holy Spirit to begin to make you sensitive to His voice. For instance, ask God to tell you what the next commercial on TV will be. Ask God to tell you what the pastor will preach about this weekend. Ask God what the next play will be in the ball game (and don't bet on the game when you do).

This all may sound too much like fortune-telling or prognostication, but it is not at all. We're not trying to predict anything; we are simply asking God to speak to us so we can learn to hear Him better. I do this sort of exercise regularly and I teach students at my training seminars to do the same.

Go with a friend to a public place such as a coffee shop or mall. Observe several people, and write down on a piece of paper what you sense God saying about them. Since this is just practice, you don't have to share it with them. Compare notes with your friend, and note any similarities in what you each were hearing.

You must first be able to successfully hear God personally or privately before you can hear God for others in a public setting. Hearing God privately will boost your confidence and prepare you to hear God for others. As you continue to practice privately, you will become more sensitive to God's Holy Spirit. Not only will you be able to hear God for yourself, but you will also be able to hear God for others. Hearing God for other people can help bring eternal change to them and draw them closer to a relationship with God.

Hearing God for Others

As we improve in hearing God, we must have a number of private successes. In fact, once we become successful in private, we will overwhelmingly want to share God's love with others. However, we can't give away what we ourselves don't have. Airline flight attendants have sound advice in this regard: "Put your own oxygen mask on before assisting someone else." If you learn to hear God for yourself, organically in the process you will grow in character. As your character increases, people will be drawn to you. As John Paul Jackson describes it, "If you have to tell people you have a revelatory gift, they will probably not believe you. But if you give them a true revelatory word from God, you will never be able to convince them that you don't." Let's have our actions, love, and character speak for us.

Humility is important in sharing the words we receive from God with people. If you are able to tell people something about themselves that was obviously revealed to you by God's Spirit, they are going to be impressed. We must always remember that whatever revelation we get is from God and not ourselves (2 Peter 1:21). If we remain humble and use our gifts to direct people to God, then God will be able to trust us and give us more revelation and greater influence and impact.

I seldom tell people I have a word from God for them. When we first begin to grow in our revelatory gifts, we may fall into the trap of wanting everyone to know we have a gift; therefore, it's important for us to work on our private successes and to let God lift us up at the appropriate time.

I do, however, look for opportunities to share God's love with people. If God does speak to me about a person, I initially assume it's not to be shared publicly, and I simply pray back to God what I just heard Him tell me. Often we aren't meant to share the revelatory words we get for people, because God just wants us to pray for that person. I have learned to ask God if I should share the word with a person; otherwise, unless I am feeling overly compelled to do so, I simply pray. Regarding strangers, particularly those outside a church setting, I make it a practice to pray for more people silently than to give revelatory words publicly.

There are times, though, when I get a revelatory word for someone, and I get the opportunity to tell him or her about it. I simply work it into the conversation, especially with food servers at restaurants. My mom was a career waitress. She worked so hard, and many people tried to lead her to Jesus in the middle of the noonday rush hour. Believe me, that's the worst time to talk to restaurant workers about their spiritual condition. Most of them have their boss breathing down their neck and have problems at home. The best thing you could ever do for them is to give them a word of encouragement and a good tip.

I offer a workshop on how to receive words of encouragement from God for people, and how to share them in nonreligious language. Words of encouragement are simply words of knowledge communicated in simple nonreligious language.

If you are going to share a revelatory word from God with someone, you must ask yourself if the person you are about to share it with views you favorably. Do you have a credible relationship with him or her? If you do not, then you are not obligated to share the word. You can have an accurate word from God, but if the person you are sharing it with doesn't trust you, then he or she probably will not be able to receive it.

This book is about using your revelatory gifts for evangelism. There is a slight difference between using your gifts inside the Church and using them outside. In both cases you should do everything out of love and good intentions. The revelation God gives you should encourage, build up, and comfort a person (1 Corinthians 14:3). The primary difference between sharing a revelatory word with another Christian and an unbeliever is how we communicate the message.

Christians may understand when we discuss prophecy, gifts of the Holy Spirit, and use phrases from the Bible. But when we use our gifts outside the Church, we must explain to people what we are doing and speak in concepts they can understand. The list of religious phrases and their nonreligious equivalents at the end of Chapter Five should assist this.

One revelatory outreach team was in a mall on a Saturday afternoon when they struck up a conversation with a hip-looking young woman. The team leader, Sonny, told her we were giving people encouraging words. The woman did not understand what that meant, so Sonny said, "We can give you a spiritual reading, but it's not psychic. It's from God." The woman agreed, and God gave Sonny a picture in his mind of the woman working with young girls and finding great satisfaction from it.

He shared this with her, and it turned out God had revealed a secret desire of her heart to work specifically with children of a certain age and development. She jumped up in her chair to a kneeling position and exclaimed, "Oh, my gosh! I have been to psychics, had my cards read, my palms read, but I have never had a Christian tell me things about my life that were accurate before!" She learned that day about a real, personal God who loves her and kids!

There are a number of ways we can use our revelatory gifts to reach people with God's love. The best way is simply to ask God to show you whom He is already drawing to Himself (John 6:65). Later on, I will discuss various ways to hear God for others. In my opinion this is one of the easiest and most effective means of evangelism. It takes a little practice, but with this approach I've seen that people are really open to hearing from God.

CHAPTER
8

IT'S REVELATION NOT FORTUNE-TELLING

Christians often ask me if receiving revelatory words for others is a New Age practice or fortune-telling. This is because many Christians have lost the understanding of how God speaks or the knowledge that God *still* speaks to people today. The media is flooded with psychic programs, streets are lined with psychic shops, and so many people believe psychics are the only ones who can get a message from the spiritual realm.

If you have ever been around real psychics, you'd see rather quickly that they can tell you things about yourself quite accurately. (However, I'm not recommending going to psychics.) So how do they do it?

As Christians we should *all* be able to hear directly from God. There are times, however, that we may need wisdom or confirmation about a serious decision. After praying and seeking God, it is appropriate to ask advice from a godly believer you can trust who is able to hear accurately from God. If believers seek to hear from God through other revelatory-gifted Christians before seeking God on their own, they are misusing God's gifts.

A woman I knew came to me with "a message from God." Quickly I realized the message was not from God; she was actually operating through a psychic spirit. She said I was going to receive a check for ten thousand dollars in the mail. When I saw that check, I would know she truly heard from God and was a prophetess. She went on to tell me that after I got the first check, I could expect another check for twenty-five thousand dollars and that I would not need to continue my job outside the ministry, because I would be taken care of by God.

About three days later, I received an unexpected check for ten thousand dollars in the mail. But the twenty-five-thousand-dollar check never came. This was not a revelatory word from God. The focus of her prophecy was to bring glory and attention to her, not to give glory to God for miraculously providing for my needs. The second part of the prophecy never came about, because it was part of Satan's plan. If I had heeded her advice, I would have become bankrupt from quitting my job and not working.

She was correct about the ten thousand dollars. How did that happen? I received the check about three days after she told me about it. The check came from out of state; therefore, it would have taken at least seven days for it to be written, signed, and mailed. At the time of her word for me, the check was already in the mail. I believe a demonic spirit saw the check being written and shared this information through a demonic network with the spirit who spoke to her. It was actually "information" not "revelation" because it had already happened. However it was presented as "revelation" of what would happen. This demonic information network is the most common way psychics and fortune-tellers receive their messages.

Most psychics are unaware that the messages they receive come through a demonic network. Many practitioners in the occult and in the New Age movement do not even believe Satan and demons exist. They do believe there are negative energy forces, but most psychics lack the spiritual discernment to know the difference. Since they do not believe in Satan, telling them they are serving the devil is *not* an effective method of reaching them.

Understanding the Source
The gift of prophecy is the ability to receive revelation or messages from God. It is not the revelation itself but the ability to receive it. There is a

big difference between a revelatory message from God and a message from a psychic or fortune-teller. The source of revelation or information makes the crucial difference.

Many psychics will tell you they hear from God, but if you ask further, most will tell you they get their messages from a spirit or a medium. Or they will tell you the tools of divination they use. Their source is not the Holy Spirit, who is the source of revelation for the Spirit-filled Christian.

Since I was a small child, I have been able to hear and communicate in the spiritual realm. For several years I had been involved in occult practice, and I heard from sources other than the Holy Spirit. I still had the ability to hear and see into the spiritual realm and have foreknowledge of events before they happened. At the time I believed my gifts were from God, but when I started going to church I was told my gifts were of the devil. This was very confusing until I found Spirit-filled Christians who helped me grow and understand the truth about spiritual gifts.

I also began to meet Christian leaders who had the gift of prophecy and who could hear God quite clearly. They shared stories about how various psychics would approach them in airports and public places and tell them they were wasting their gifts by being Christian. When I heard John Paul Jackson speak on the difference between a psychic and a prophet,[1] the pieces of my life started to fit together and make sense. John Paul had studied spiritual gifts for a number of years, and he brought clarity to the subject through Bible teaching. He explained that our spiritual gifts come from God, and unless we give our lives to Jesus Christ, we can have a gift from God that is pointed in the wrong direction or is being used for purposes other than those God intended.

This happened in the life of Samson, who used his God-given strength for his own gain (Judges 15). The prophet Balaam was known to use his gift for sorcery (Numbers 24). King Saul, although anointed by the prophet Samuel, turned his gifts away from God's purposes and ended up consulting a medium for direction (1 Samuel 28).

People can have spiritual gifts from God that were given at their birth. Jeremiah, while still in his mother's womb, was gifted as a prophet (Jeremiah 1:5). David realized that his destiny in God emerged while he was still an infant (Psalm 22:9). Timothy, on the other hand, received his gift as the apostle Paul laid his hands on him and prayed (2 Timothy 1:6).

John Paul Jackson made an important observation: God is the only one who has the ability to create gifts . . . or anything, for that matter. (The enemy can only "create" havoc!) Satan is not a creator. He was actually created by God and can only steal and counterfeit what God has already created.

God is the Creator and Giver of all good things. The Hebrew word for "create" is *barah* and means "something out of nothing." This word is used only in reference to God and His activity.

> For by him [Jesus] all things were created: things in heaven and on earth, visible and invisible, whether thrones or powers or rulers or authorities; all things were created by him and for him.
> —Colossians 1:16

Gifts come only from God.

> Every good and perfect gift is from above, coming down from the Father of the heavenly lights, who does not change like shifting shadows.
> —James 1:17

However, Satan has made counterfeiting and distorting what God has already created an art and a science, so if people with gifts from God choose not to use those gifts for God, then Satan can persuade or deceive these people to use their gifts for other means.

> So Moses and Aaron went to Pharaoh and did just as the LORD commanded. Aaron threw his staff down in front of Pharaoh and his officials, and it became a snake. Pharaoh then summoned wise men and sorcerers, and the Egyptian magicians also did the same things by their secret arts . . ."
> Exodus 7:10–11

Thus all gifts come from God; the messages or revelations (the transmission of the gifts) can be from a source other than God's Holy Spirit.

John Paul Jackson teaches that to understand the different sources of revelation, we need to look at how it all began in the Garden of Eden.

And the LORD God made all kinds of trees grow out of the ground—trees that were pleasing to the eye and good for food. In the middle of the garden were the tree of life and the tree of the knowledge of good and evil.
—Genesis 2:9

There were two trees in the Garden. One was the Tree of Life. If Adam and Eve ate from it, they would live forever (Genesis 3:22). The other was the Tree of the Knowledge of Good and Evil. If Adam and Eve ate from it, they would die (Genesis 2:17). Satan was present in the Garden and tempted them to eat from the Tree of the Knowledge of Good and Evil.

What was the temptation? The fruit looked good, and Satan said it would make them be like God (Genesis 3:5). This is the New Age message—we are all gods. But it's not a new message at all.

The Tree of the Knowledge of Good and Evil represents the soulish side of creation, while the Tree of Life represents the spirit. In the Bible, the Tree of Life appears again in the New Holy City of God, the New Jerusalem (Revelation 22:2).[2]

The two trees in the Garden represent the two sources of revelation. One source is the soul, and the other is the spirit. The Greek word for "soul" is *psuche*, which is where we get the word *psychic*. Throughout the Bible, we see a conflict between these two sources: the soul and the spirit.

Removing the Fear

How can you tell if you are operating through the correct source? If you have given your life to Jesus Christ and you sincerely desire to be filled with and led by the Holy Spirit, then you have the seed of God's Spirit within you. When you ask God to give you a word of knowledge or a prophetic word, it is important that you do so through the Holy Spirit.

Unless you were previously involved in the occult, you probably do not need to be concerned about operating through other spirits. However, if you were involved in the occult, you can pray a simple prayer to close any doors from the past, allowing God's Holy Spirit to flow through you. It is easy to break any ties to the past, and I'd recommend doing so with a pastor, leader, or trusted Christian friend. After you have closed the doors to the past through prayer, it is best not to focus on the past and not to worry about getting words from other sources.

Hearing God consistently takes time and practice. The more the Holy Spirit has control of our lives, the more accurately and consistently we are able to hear God. For most Christians, the most difficult part of hearing God is not the inability to distinguish God's words versus demonic words; rather, it is discerning what is from God versus our soul—our own thoughts, ideas, intentions, and emotions. This discernment comes with practice. The more you practice, the easier it is to know whether it is God who is speaking.

As we step out and begin to get revelatory words of encouragement for others, always remember that God is the One who created revelatory messages, including dreams, visions, and the supernatural.

Dreams and visions make up over one third of the Bible. The birth of Jesus was announced through a dream. Paul and Peter were both guided by dreams. Why then might some Christians view dream interpretation as a New Age practice? Many in the West have not understood the importance of dreams as a revelatory tool and have not valued this wonderful mode through which God speaks to us.

The Bible is full of strange and unusual supernatural experiences that are too often relegated to the realm of the paranormal; we have not made room for God to be God. God loves to perform signs and wonders, and we need to make room in our lives for God to display His supernatural majesty—to prove He is God. If through our fears and misconceptions we try to put God in our little box, we won't experience the full and exciting spiritual life He intends for us. However, every unusual and strange occurrence is not necessarily from God. As 2 Thessalonians 2:9 (NKJV) warns: "The coming of the lawless one is according to the working of Satan, with all power, signs, and lying wonders"; therefore, wisdom and discernment are needed to distinguish between the genuine and the counterfeit because Satan will always try to steal, pervert, distort, or destroy what is God's.

Some Christians have become accustomed to God's power and presence being demonstrated in church to people in need of Him. But outside on the streets, I have found it to be an even more powerful way to show God's love and touch those who don't yet know Him. If you pray for a person in front of a movie theater or in a grocery store and the person gets physically healed or can feel oppression lift off him or her, it is a dramatic demonstration of this person encountering the one true God. Jesus said:

> "But if I drive out demons by the Spirit of God, then the kingdom of God has come upon you."
> —Matthew 12:28

Once I was leading an evangelistic outreach at a New Age convention with more than a hundred booths of well-known New Age groups. My team was in a booth across from the Kabala Center and next to a group of witches. We were offering free dream interpretations and selling John Paul Jackson's *Moments with God* dream journal. By the end of the convention, my team had given over two hundred and fifty dream interpretations and had prayed for many people. We had four major prayer encounters in which the person being prayed for felt demonic spirits leave his or her body. We used our process evangelism skills, conversing with people at their level of receptivity.

One woman who had come for dream interpretation shared that she was overwhelmed by the peace she felt in our presence, and she wept as we prayed with her. The encounter lasted for more than an hour. Before leaving our booth, she invited us to come to her New Age bookstore and do a dream interpretation event. A month later our dream team arrived, and she met them at the door saying, "Do you see all of this stuff?"—she pointed to the items stocked in her store. "Nothing in here has touched me as deeply as you did at the convention!" Since then, our dream teams have been frequenting New Age bookstores, coffeehouses, and events, developing relationships with employees and patrons, who often express surprise that Christians can hear God so clearly and are stunned that we want to befriend them.

God will use each of us in unexpected situations if we simply watch for Him, allow Him to work, and remove the limitations from our expectations. Many Christians have been taught to fear and avoid New Age and occult people. However, if every area of our lives is submitted to God through the Holy Spirit, we need not fear. Of course, we want to be wise and careful, only going to places where God leads us, but we always need to remember we serve a great and powerful God.

. . . the one who is in you is greater than the one who is in the world.
—1 John 4:4

We have God's unlimited power through the Holy Spirit, but we must also have the character of Jesus and His love for people. Jesus says:

"But I tell you: Love your enemies and pray for those who persecute you."
—Matthew 5:44

Jesus' followers are to love and pray for people who do not know Him—people in other religions, the occult, or the New Age.

When we take our dream teams into New Age events, we do not walk around praying for psychics to lose their power or to close down. They can feel when we pray this way; they get agitated at our presence and want nothing to do with us. Instead we ask God to bless them and draw them to Himself. When we do this, they are much more open to talking with us.

I once knew a psychic whom God was drawing to Himself. She was nervous about becoming a Christian, because it would mean she would lose her job—tarot-card reading, which was her main source of income—the only job she'd had since she was young. At that particular time I thought it best to bless her and ask God to provide so much income that she would not have to work or could find a new source of income.

I have found that when we pray and bless those around us, they are much more open to interacting with us; they are even open to receiving prayer. We have had reports that some psychics lose their power when we walk by their booths, but this is not from our praying against them; it comes from the deluge of God's love and presence surrounding us.

When this happens, psychics are often drawn to us because the God we serve is obviously stronger than the god they serve.

Jesus and His disciples used spiritual gifts to help open people's eyes and draw them to God. Until recently many Christians have not understood how to hear God, so they have not been able to allow His power free reign in them to draw people to Jesus. As we begin to use the Holy Spirit's gifts in our everyday lives and allow God liberty to do with us whatever He wills, we will see and experience amazing things. Then people will want to know this God we serve.

SECTION
III

EXCITING WAYS
to SHARE
GOD'S LOVE

CHAPTER 9

AN APPOINTMENT
with GOD

W hen I first began to lead evangelism workshops and out-reaches only a few people would come. This would disappoint me, because Christians did not seem to value evangelism. One person's feedback was: "Oh no, not another method. There can't be another new method; I've tried them all." Sadly I had to agree with him. On the subject of evangelism, it seemed Christians had heard it all.

I've always felt uncomfortable about making evangelism an event and not a lifestyle. Approaching strangers has never been fun for me. Occasionally I will run into people who seem to be ready to talk about God. They might reveal some details in their life and end up asking me about God. I only wish all my encounters were that smooth and easy. In actuality, there's no reason why we can't regularly engage in positive, fruitful evangelistic encounters.

Every day we come into contact with hundreds of people who do not know God's love. Imagine if we could hear God tell us who He is drawing. When we do, my teams and I seem to encounter people who are really open to talking more about God!

This exciting encounter happened during one of our prophetic evangelism outreaches at a New England shopping mall:

Sarah entered the mall on a rainy Saturday afternoon and headed to Sears to pick something up for her mom. She had no idea she was about to have an appointment with God.

A small group of Christians who had just taken a course on how to give people words of encouragement had gone to the mall to practice what they'd just learned. The group's leader was recalling a recent dream in which she met a woman and prayed for the healing of her ears.

Suddenly Sarah walked by. The group stopped her, explaining they had just taken a class and wanted to practice giving her an encouraging word. Sarah was a little hesitant, but she agreed. They gave a few positive encouraging words. Just as Sarah was about to thank them and continue on with her shopping, the group's leader, Mary, told her they also believed in divine healing and wanted to know whether there was anything they could pray for her about. Surprised, Sarah remarked, "I can't believe you asked me that!" She proceeded to tell the group about her partially deaf right ear, which had recently interfered with her ability to get a job she really wanted. She had just prayed, "God, it would be really cool if you would have someone come along and offer to pray for my ear." The group was more than delighted to oblige. They placed their hands on Sarah's ears and prayed for her in the middle of the mall. At that time Sarah was not healed (that we know of), but she walked away knowing that God really cares for her.

Such encounters should not surprise us because God wants to use us when we make ourselves available to Him.

For we are God's workmanship, created in Christ Jesus to do good works, which God prepared in advance for us to do.
—Ephesians 2:10

Divine Appointments
We call such encounters "divine appointments," a specific time at which an individual or a group has an encounter with God. It involves being in the right place at the right time for God to show up through His Holy

Spirit in a special way.

Philip experienced this phenomenon, recorded in Acts 8:26–27:

> Now an angel of the Lord said to Philip, "Go south to the road—the desert road—that goes down from Jerusalem to Gaza." So he started out, and on his way he met an Ethiopian eunuch.

The Ethiopian eunuch Philip met was reading a prophecy about the coming of the Messiah from the book of Isaiah. Philip asked if he understood what he was reading, which opened the door to a conversation culminating in the man's baptism. Just as the angel in this account advised Philip exactly where to go, we too can be directed by God to find people whom God wants to encourage. Remember, prophetic evangelism means not only using our revelatory gifts to share God's love but also to know whom to speak with and where to meet them.

Quite often God will direct our revelatory and dream teams by words of knowledge, prophecy, or dreams sharing exactly where to go on their outreaches. Occasionally they are given people's names or shown people's faces before ever meeting them.

One afternoon, leading a prophetic evangelism team in a mall, I asked God where we should go. The next moment I looked up and saw a sign that read SEARS pointing to the right and immediately felt God reply, "Seers go to the right." We headed toward Sears. Within fifteen minutes after setting up, a line of people waited eagerly to learn what God was saying about them. We didn't display any signs or distribute flyers; we simply asked people if we could practice "hearing God" on their behalf. After another fifteen minutes passed I looked up to see one of our team members leading a store manager in a prayer to commit her life to Christ.

The Bible overflows with divine appointments recounting sudden encounters with God changing lives. For example, the ungodly king Nebuchadnezzar had a troubling dream which no one could interpret except Daniel. Daniel not only rehashed the king's dream for him (the king hadn't confided in anyone about the details of the dream) but also offered the dream's interpretation. The dream's impact turned the king into a worshipper of the God of the Israelites.

> Then King Nebuchadnezzar fell prostrate before Daniel and paid him honor and ordered that an offering and incense be presented to him. The king said to Daniel, "Surely your God is the God of gods and the Lord of kings and a revealer of mysteries, for you were able to reveal this mystery."
> —Daniel 2:46–47

Another dramatic evangelistic encounter happened to the tax collector Zacchaeus, who was greatly disliked. Zacchaeus climbed a tree, desperate to see Jesus. When Jesus came by, He looked up at Zacchaeus and announced He would stay at Zacchaeus' house. As a result Zacchaeus became a believer and repaid the money he had appropriated unrighteously (Luke 19:1–10). Jesus announced, "Today salvation has come to this house, because this man, too, is a son of Abraham" (Luke 19:9).

Listen for the Holy Spirit's direction in where to look for people He has been preparing. If you are in the right place at the right time, the result will be a divine encounter.

One of the most amazing experiences I've ever witnessed illustrates how God guides us to people who need Him. A small church in the United Kingdom invited Streams Ministries to do a dream team outreach at the 2002 Commonwealth Games in Manchester, England. The pastor had read an article in *Charisma* magazine about how Streams dream teams ministered at the 2002 Winter Olympics.[1] He was impressed by God to bring us to reach people in England similarly.

Streams Dream Team members hailed from different states throughout the United States; they had not worked together before the trip to England. Upon our arrival in the city, we assembled to pray for direction and discovered that several team members had been dreaming about Manchester though they had never been there. Brenda from Connecticut related that before the trip she'd dreamed she was in downtown Manchester, England, and there saw a particular building, behind which was a parked car with AUSTIN POWERS written on both sides. Later that day the church's pastor was driving downtown with a team en route to our first outreach event in an area where athletes and spectators were most likely to be found. To the group's surprise Brenda began screaming to stop as her mind flashed back to her dream. "Suddenly I was in my dream, where I had walked those very streets," recalled Brenda. "It was the wildest thing I'd ever experienced." Scott from New Jersey, who was also in the car with Brenda, had dreamed about a building adjacent to the library.

I asked the pastor if there was a library nearby. When he confirmed there was and pointed it out, I asked him to drive behind it. "It was an unnerving experience," explained Scott. "It felt like I'd literally been there in my dream a year earlier."

We asked the pastor to drop us off near the two buildings that had appeared in Brenda's and Scott's dreams. Sure enough, we immediately began to meet people who were spiritually hungry and very open to discussing God. Several people gave their lives to Jesus as we interpreted their dreams and gave them prophetic words from God. At the time, I thought to myself: *This must have been how Philip felt when the angel directed him to meet the Ethiopian eunuch. Can it get any better than this?* It did!

To our amazement, we found a black taxi with AUSTIN POWERS on its side. That was a sign to us: We were in the right place at the right time, and God was planning to orchestrate a divine appointment.

The highlight of our trip happened on the final night of our outreach, as team members gathered at the town center to exchange goodbyes. Jacquelyne, a dream team member from Scotland, confided her disappointment about not meeting someone named Martin, whom she had dreamed about and which of all our dreams and directive words from God, was the only one that hadn't transpired. Then suddenly, in an astounding turn of events, two drunk young men approached our group inquiring what was going on, seeing thirty people standing there hugging and biding one another farewell.

One of the men noticed our sign offering free dream interpretation and asked if we would interpret a dream of his. He described his dream; we gave him the interpretation, and he began to leave. Since our practice is to get people's first names for our prayer list and we had neglected to ascertain his, I shouted out after him, "Hey, what's your name?" He replied, "My name is Martin." Everyone in the group went wild. He looked at us like we were crazy as everyone yelled, "Martin!" Then

Jacquelyne stepped forward and shared her dream with him.

In her dream Jacquelyne had met a man named Martin who had recently broken off a relationship, changed his hairstyle, and was considering attending school. Martin confirmed that everything she'd mentioned was indeed true, stunned to discover God knew about his life and was calling out to him. Martin asked us to pray for him; he instantly sobered up and gave his life to Jesus. One of the dream team members from Manchester worked with Martin, so she would follow up with him.

Can you imagine the possibilities if Christians everywhere began asking God to direct them to those ready for the touch of His love? I believe God is calling us to plug in to the Holy Spirit network for instruction in partnering together to spread the good news of God's love for the world.

CHAPTER 10

THE POWER *of* ENCOURAGING WORDS

M ost people have preconceived ideas about how Christians should look and act. Unfortunately these stereotypes do not justly portray what Christianity is really about. People are often surprised to learn that God wants to speak to them, and that Christians can accurately hear God for them.

When we tell people what we believe God is telling us about them and it rings true, their first response is usually, "Are you psychic?" This is because our society has lost track of how or even that God speaks to us. Thus, the Church has allowed New Agers and psychics to become the most popular means of seeking direction in life, but in reality God is the only giver of true direction for life.

Psychic hotlines are a multibillion dollar industry. This should provide a clue about the strong demand for direction people look for from a source beyond themselves; this only underscores just how sad it is that although this yearning is so innate and common to humanity, most people around the globe don't know they can obtain specific guidance and direction from their Creator through Christians.

When I first began searching for new ways to convey the love for people that God was growing in me, I heard that several Christian groups were beginning to use revelatory gifts successfully in evangelism. Drawn further to this arena, I attended several prophetic evangelism conferences and was involved in some outreaches. I was stunned to discover people's interest in hearing from God, and I was equally and pleasantly surprised to discover how easy it was to hear God for others once I got over my fear of rejection and just took the plunge. I also found that attendees at these conferences were highly gifted Christians who operated in revelatory gifts regularly—only approximately ten percent of church members in general understand and regularly use their spiritual gifts.

My first prophetic evangelism training was with Patricia King of Extreme Prophetic Ministries. At her conference I went on an outreach led by Stacey Campbell of Revival Now Ministries and I was part of a team offering "spiritual readings" (prophetic words) at a popular juice store in downtown Kelowna, British Columbia. A young woman approached our table and sat down. We told her we were Christians— not psychics—and believed that God wants to speak to people. We asked her what she might be interested in knowing. "I want to know if I should marry the guy I am with," she replied. Now, marriage is an area we tend to avoid giving prophetic words about, but since we asked her what she wanted, we felt pressure to answer her needs. We closed our eyes briefly and sought God about her situation.

In my mind an image of a rose appeared. Just as I saw the rose, the team leader said, "God sees you as a rose" and continued describing how special the young woman was to God. Then it was my turn. "Roses are used at weddings and funerals," I told her. "What do you think this means about your relationship with this guy?" Hearing my words, the woman burst into tears and responded, "I know I'm not supposed to marry him!" We went on to pray with her, and she really felt she'd heard from God.

Afterwards I began teaching people at my church how to receive words from God for others. When put on the spot, however, most were unable to receive these revelations in public. Thus began my search for ways to teach Christians how to do this type of evangelism.

While many Christians still share their faith, for the most part they are not overly excited about doing so. They become discouraged after trying to share their faith, because most people erect a wall of defense when you discuss their spiritual needs. Nonetheless, people need God and they need to know He cares about even the most seemingly trivial aspects of their lives. After personally experiencing several positive encounters using revelatory evangelism, I became convinced this is an effective way to reach an entire generation.

An Experience that Changed My Life

A few years ago my life was forever changed when I began to lead prophetic evangelism outreaches at conferences. I would offer a short teaching on instances of prophetic evangelism in the Bible, and then we would practice receiving words of knowledge for one another. Next, we would travel to a public place for a series of Holy Spirit-led encounters. It was a lot of fun, and God used us to touch and pray for hundreds of people.

At one of my first conferences, several teams gathered in the food court of a shopping mall. Three teams felt impressed by God to talk with various individuals whom they approached and struck up conversations with. Interestingly, each of these individuals had been thinking, God, if you are real, send someone to talk with me. The teams were stoked and exhilarated!

Another team approached a man who looked lonely. Telling him they had taken a class in giving people encouraging words, the group asked the man if they could practice on him. Within minutes of talking with our team members, the man began to share his feelings of emptiness and ended up inviting Jesus into his life.

That day fourteen people came to Jesus, and several people were physically healed! I returned home and began to study prophetic evangelism more deeply, and explored more by going on outreaches. Later I developed a workshop geared to teaching Christians how to hear God-given words of encouragement for people and communicate them in nonreligious language. In the workshop, we focus on offering encouragement that tries to build people up and validate their worth to God. Then we venture to a public place, asking God to lead us to those He wants us to encourage. In many ways it seems too easy. We simply ask God to speak to us, trust our God-inspired hunches, and communicate in everyday language what we feel God is saying.

At one outreach a woman was told, "When I look at you I see some-one who is a natural-born encourager; people feel safe to share their problems with you." She smiled and replied, "You're right, I'm a coun-selor. How do you know this about me?" We responded, "We're learn-ing to hear from God. We're not psychics; we are Christians. But we are probably not like many Christians you have met." Most people are stunned to learn that Christians can truly hear from God.

Furthermore, most people don't have a clue that God wants to encourage them; in fact, many believe He is angry with them. So, when we offer words of encouragement, people let their walls down and are very open to talking more about God.

We try to tailor our approach to the community in which our event is taking place because we want people to encounter God. We've found the more we meet people where they are at and speak in language as familiar to them and nonreligious as possible, the better success we have in avoiding having them erect defenses and close down to us . . . and thereby being fully able to touch them with God's loving message. Overall people are spiritually open.

> But everyone who prophesies speaks to men for their strengthening, *encouragement* and comfort.
> —1 Corinthians 14:3, Italics mine

Our language and the style of these outreaches therefore vary with the environment we're trying to reach; whereas in some secular venues, we tell people that we are giving encouraging words. In others, we might claim to be doing "spiritual readings," which does not mean "New Age." Spiritual readings are God's revelatory words for people communicated in straightforward language so they can receive and have an inkling of God's heart.

Todd Bentley of Fresh Fire Ministries reports these results with prophetic evangelism in malls in South Korea:[1]

> Hundreds converged on mall floors doing "God readings" (prophecy over unbelievers). One hundred and seventy-four people were

saved in two hours. We hung up a sign in Korean that said, FREE SPIRITUAL READINGS. In the food court we set up six tables, with two people and a translator at each. We gave prophetic words for two hours, while hundreds of others went throughout the mall praying and gathering the lost. Several of the souls saved were Buddhists.

Brent Lokker, Pastor of Blazing Fire Church in Dublin, California, sent me this report about his church's use of encouraging words:

Doug Addison taught us to hear God's voice for ordinary people as a means of encouraging them. We also learned how to talk about spiritual issues without sounding weird or religious.

At the end of Doug's prophetic evangelism workshop, our teams went to a courtyard, various coffee shops, and a shopping mall to practice what we had learned. We saw God's love and power working through us to pierce the hearts of many people. We knew this was something we had to keep doing!

Every Friday night since then, we have returned to the same courtyard, which is a hangout for young people who seem open and hungry for spiritual things. One night we spoke prophetic encouragement to a young Hindu man. He was profoundly touched by the words. Another night we shared some truth about Jesus with a group of ten teenagers.

One boy had just broken his arm, and the doctors were waiting for the swelling to subside before they made a cast. We explained that God could heal it right now. His eyes grew wide with surprise as the team prayed. He began to move his fingers and even made a fist saying he couldn't do this before. Much excitement filled the air!

On three different occasions, people with crutches were instantly healed! One night God healed eight different people from the local high school football team; several of them gave their lives to Jesus. We have met with a pregnant teenager, people contemplating suicide, and even some Muslim families.

Our outreach continues to grow. A few months ago, we started interpreting dreams and found that the Lord often uses dreams to speak with those who don't know Him yet. As we listen to their dreams, we help them make a connection to God.

We also have a second group that takes food to the homeless and shares words of encouragement with them. Although the homeless often receive food, it's rare for anyone to take time to listen and speak encouragement over their lives.

In just over a year, a small number of Christians have represented God in new ways to many people outside the church. We will never be the same!

Revelatory outreaches have the potential for profoundly affecting people who don't know God with love. An outreach could happen on a Saturday at your local shopping mall, where many hurting and lonely people go to kill time and try to feel better. We don't all have to occupy the office of an evangelist to walk through a mall asking God to point out to us individuals needing encouragement. Imagine the possibilities if we became intentional with our faith and trusted the Holy Spirit to guide us in the harvest He desires.

CHAPTER
11

DREAM
TEAMS

One cold Saturday afternoon Rob and his wife, Kathy, went to the local coffee shop for some warm java. They struck up a conversation with two women at the next table. Rob mentioned that he and Kathy had just returned from the Sundance Film Festival, where they had interpreted dreams for people. He asked whether the women had any dreams they wanted interpreted. The women nearly fell out of their chairs with excitement; one said they had just been discussing a dream she'd had the night before and were on their way to buy a dream book to interpret its meaning.

Rob and Kathy revealed her dream's meaning, then the meaning of another dream, and then another. Two more women joined their friends, and Rob and Kathy interpreted their dreams as well.

Tears flowed from several of the women as God revealed their hearts' secrets. They all happened to be childhood friends now in their thirties who had grown up going to church but never really connected with God. Rob and Kathy proclaimed, "The Jesus of your youth is real and bigger than you know." The women thanked them and claimed they were really encouraged to reconnect with God.

This is a typical encounter for those who have been trained to interpret dreams from a biblical perspective. Some people believe that dreams are psychological and can only be interpreted by a psychologist or psychiatrist. Even psychics who interpret dreams are using methods popularized by psychotherapists. Since a significant portion of the Bible pertains to dreams and visions, we can familiarize ourselves with God's hidden language to help unlock a dream's secret meaning to people's understanding.

Biblical Dream Interpretation

As I previously mentioned I first heard about dream team evangelism from John Paul Jackson of Streams Ministries. My wife and I took his courses on dreams through the Streams Institute for Spiritual Development (ISD). John Paul has studied dreams and visions for more than twenty-five years. He noticed that if you took the popular dream interpretation methods used today—Freudian, Jungian, or Gestalt—and applied them to dreams in the Bible, you would not arrive with the same interpretation given in Scripture. This indicates that these methods are not accurate and will give you an incorrect interpretation.

When I took the ISD courses, John Paul related how his interns and students who had taken his courses walked into a large bookstore chain that was advertising tarot-card readings and various New Age seminars. One former intern approached the bookstore's manager inquiring whether he and his friends could offer a dream interpretation seminar. First the manager demanded they interpret one of her dreams, which until then no one had been able to interpret.

They went into her office and listened to her rehash the dream. As John Paul's interns interpreted her dream, she began to weep uncontrollably, sliding out of her chair and falling to the floor. When her composure returned, she ensured an opportunity for them to hold a dream interpretation seminar at the bookstore.

They were booked on one of the slowest nights of the month. Within six months sales shot up to their highest on the nights when the Streams Dream Team was there. The team even had to help a few people to their cars because they were so deeply moved after having a dream interpreted. Letters began arriving at Streams from area churches telling about visitors who had given their lives to Jesus after having dreams interpreted at the bookstore.

The reports about the Streams Dream Teams excited me greatly and confirmed my assessment about using dream interpretation to reach people with God's love. Later I joined Streams Ministries as the National Dream Team Coordinator and began teaching people how to interpret dreams and use dream interpretation as a means of evangelism.

My first dream team outreach was at the 2002 Winter Olympics in Salt Lake City, Utah. Team members flew in from around the United States to interpret dreams at the Olympics. Outreaches were focused on restaurants, coffeehouses, and even bars surrounding the hotels. We used the method we had learned in the classroom and relied heavily on the Holy Spirit to help us with the dream's meaning. We kept it simple and interpreted what the dream meant. If the people seemed open to talking, we would tell them what we felt God was conveying through the dreams. Since dreams are often spiritual, we would use the dream interpretation as an entrée into discussing spiritual issues in their lives.

One of our dream teams during the Olympics was in a New Age restaurant, near a table of college-age guys curious about what we were doing, so we interpreted several of their dreams. They seemed open, so we delved a little further in the conversation. Addressing one of the young men, a team member declared, "This dream indicates that you have a spiritual destiny and that there is a greater purpose in your life." The man eyed the team leader intently and agreed that he knew there was something missing from his life.

They talked about God, and his spiritual needs, and just before they left the team leader got a word of knowledge for the man. He told him, "You are going to find your spirituality through the Twelve Steps [Alcoholics Anonymous]. The man announced, "Dude, my brother just got in A.A. and he is now a man of God!" God used that encounter to help guide a wandering young man with a great calling from God to be in ministry.

Symbolic Language of Dreams
Most people do not doubt that God can speak to us through dreams, but many Christians feel uneasy about dream interpretation as a means of evangelism. Some may argue that Jesus never used this style of evangelism. My response to that is Jesus never gave out tracts the way many Christians do today. Just because Jesus did not do it does not mean that

we cannot. Jesus never stood up and spoke to philosophers the way Paul did on Mars Hill (Acts 17), but that was effective. The apostle Paul was very good at recognizing how to communicate with different types of people. He claimed to gear his approach differently in order to win various sorts of people to Jesus Christ (1 Corinthians 9:19–22).

Jesus taught people through parables—stories with a deeper meaning. He admonished His disciples that they must be able to interpret parables and understand symbolic thinking in order to uncover the mysteries of the Kingdom (Matthew 13:10–15). Dreams are symbolic and are basically night parables. The apostle Paul talks about the interpretation of tongues (1 Corinthians 12:10). The principle of interpretation lines up with the Bible, so interpreting dreams, using the Holy Spirit as a counselor, is a safe practice.

Even though we do not see Jesus doing dream interpretations, we do see Joseph and Daniel interpreting dreams for secular people (Genesis 40–41; Daniel 2). In fact, King Nebuchadnezzar was so desperate to have his dream interpreted that he "motivated" his court's wise men by decreeing execution for any who couldn't interpret it. When they suggested Nebuchadnezzar summon Daniel to interpret the dream, Daniel went home and informed his friends Hananiah, Mishael, and Azariah (Daniel 2:17). That night God gave Daniel both an account of the king's dream as well as its interpretation. When Daniel repeated it all to him the next day, the king fell on his face acknowledging, "Surely your God is the God of gods and the Lord of kings and a revealer of mysteries, for you were able to reveal this mystery" (Daniel 2:47). A dream correctly interpreted will prompt people to worship the living God. Notice that first the king consulted the astrologers and wise men of Babylon, and none of them could manage to interpret the dream (Daniel 2). This is because God reveals the interpretation through His servants.

> The man without the Spirit does not accept the things that come from the Spirit of God, for they are foolishness to him, and he cannot understand them, because they are spiritually discerned.
> —1 Corinthians 2:14

Not all dreams are from God. Some dreams arise from a person's own soul, and some may be sparked by the demonic realm.

People everywhere dream, and many of these dreams are from God. On our outreaches people often tell us no one could accurately interpret their dreams before. God is waiting for Christians to step out and give them the dream's interpretation.

Learning to interpret dreams isn't easy. Since dreams are often symbolic rather than literal, it's important to study the dreams contained in the Bible, because as you study the dream symbols, metaphors, and parables there, you will begin to recognize God's hidden language. Interpreting dreams requires practice and reliance on the Holy Spirit to speak to the interpreter. It is not as easy as looking up the meanings of dream symbols in a book; dream symbols or elements may vary from dream to dream or from dreamer to dreamer.

Our dream teams frequent popular coffee shops, bookstore chains, and New Age events around the world. We don't advertise up front that we are Christians because otherwise the people we want to reach would not talk with us. Instead we use dream interpretation as a means of initiating interactions with people who would normally steer clear of us. We are not deceiving them in any way; rather, we are providing them with a legitimate interpretation of their dreams. Once we unlock their dreams' meaning or tell them information only God could know about them, they are usually very open to finding out more about God and are convinced, perhaps, of their need of Him.

Although we are covert in order to get into conversations with people, we will identify ourselves as Christians—especially once they are deeply touched. We simply say, "We're Christians who are learning to hear God. But we are probably not like any Christians you have met before." Their reply is usually "I'll say. I never knew Christians could do this." Then their next response is "I never realized that God wanted to speak to me."

Pastors and church leaders have come to dream team events unaware that we are Christians. When we confront them as to why they would be willing to venture to have readings from alleged New Agers, many admit they never knew Christians could interpret dreams. They had been haunted by a dream and just had to know what it meant.

John Paul Jackson reported about a dream team encounter in Poland that Recie Saunders, Streams National Ministry Teams Director, had:

> After one of our classes in Poland, Recie joined some students for dinner at a nearby restaurant. While they were at the restaurant, a man at the next table began taunting the group. As the night progressed, it became clear that the man was trying to pick a fight, and the students were doing their best to avoid an incident.
>
> Feeling impressed by the Lord, Recie asked the man if he had a dream that he didn't understand. Startled, the man said, "Yes, I had one just the other night. I was in a dark prison and I was stabbing and killing men. I was really enjoying it." Recie asked if the dream was in color or if it was a dark dream; the man indicated it was a dark dream. Recognizing that the demonic realm had given the dream, Recie "turned around" the dream to give it a positive slant. He told the man that while the enemy was trying to make him a "life taker," God had created him to be a "life giver."
>
> The atmosphere in the room grew thick with the Holy Spirit's presence. In a poignant moment, God instantly gave Recie a word of knowledge about an event that happened to the man at the age of seven. Because of this event, the man had become miserable, angry, and violent. Hearing those words, the man bowed his head and began to weep, along with everyone else at both tables. He couldn't understand why he was crying—he had never cried!
>
> Explaining that he had been in and out of prison several times, the man had recently resigned himself to the darkness that he thought would follow him for the rest of his life. Through his tears, the man told his friends, "Everything this man has said is the truth." Then, looking at Recie, he said, "My friends and I met tonight to burglarize a house. If the owners tried to stop us, we would have badly hurt them." Looking at his friends with a new conviction he announced, "Now we are not going to do that." [1]

It is amazing how God is using dream team evangelism to touch people for Jesus. If we step out, God will be with us as we take His light into the darkest areas, and when we do, we will find God's light shining all the brighter.

CHAPTER 12

POWER ENCOUNTERS

During His ministry Jesus brought the Kingdom of God to earth (Matthew 3:2), engendering a clash between the powers of darkness and the God of light. Today whenever God's Kingdom is present, a conflict between those powers ensues.

As we carry the presence of the Holy Spirit, people encounter God and often experience this conflict, the most common manifestation of which is unbelief. Most people do not believe Jesus' message; therefore, we must all the more intensely demonstrate God's love and shatter their unbelief.

The apostle Paul states throughout his writings that he relayed Jesus' message not *just* with words but with the power and demonstration of the Holy Spirit (1 Corinthians 2:1–5). Paul viewed his ministry to the Gentiles accordingly:

> I will not venture to speak of anything except what Christ has accomplished through me in leading the Gentiles to obey God by what I have said and done—by the power of signs and miracles, through the power of the Spirit.
> —Romans 15:18–19

Transformed Lives

When we proclaim the good news of Jesus Christ, it is not good news unless power is present to transform a person's life. One reason why Christianity is losing its influence in America is because most Christians do not appropriate and consistently operate in God's power. Therefore, because the world is not seeing God-talk translated into action nowadays, it concludes that God stopped communing with us and performing miracles after the death of the first apostles. In contrary, Jesus promised:

> Most assuredly, I say to you, he who believes in Me, the works that I do he will do also; and *greater* works than these he will do . . .
> —John 14:12, Italics mine

Power encounters occur when Jesus' followers bring God's power and presence through the Holy Spirit to a person who does not believe or is trapped in darkness by evil forces. Encounters of this sort are plentiful throughout the Bible.

> When he [Jesus] arrived at the other side in the region of the Gadarenes, two demon-possessed men coming from the tombs met him. They were so violent that no one could pass that way. "What do you want with us, Son of God?" they shouted. "Have you come here to torture us before the appointed time?" Some distance from them a large herd of pigs was feeding. The demons begged Jesus, "If you drive us out, send us into the herd of pigs." He said to them, "Go!" So they came out and went into the pigs, and the whole herd rushed down the steep bank into the lake and died in the water.
> —Matthew 8:28–32

Although this account of Jesus driving demons into the pigs appears quite dramatic, we do what we've seen the Son doing. If we encountered afflicted ones in need of healing, and God healed them through our prayers, we would indeed be expelling darkness from their lives.

Ambassadors of Divine Authority

Prior to embarking on an outreach at a busy mall, several members of one of our prophetic teams had a sensation of "hot tingling hands," so the leaders directed them to search for sick people to pray for. The team was drawn to a woman with a withered hand who was walking with a limp. They introduced themselves as part of a group that believes in divine healing and asked if they could pray for her, to which she agreed. As they prayed her withered hand opened and her foot straightened! Now, that was a power encounter! She was so excited by this display of God's power that she prayed and invited Jesus into her life. The woman had not only been sick and in need of salvation, she also confessed she had been quite discouraged and despondent. This divine touch instantly healed her emotionally, physically, and spiritually.

Delegated Authority

As we enter public places to interact and pray with people, we need to know that we are instruments of divine power and wield authority as divine ambassadors. Through Jesus we have power and authority to heal and cast out demons in His name (Luke 9:1), an authority similar to police officers who stop someone and slap the person with a ticket for breaking the law. In the same way that earthly ambassadors are protected by "diplomatic immunity," we must learn to use the weapons of spiritual warfare (2 Corinthians 10:4–6; Ephesians 6:10–20) and render ourselves protected by "spiritual diplomatic immunity" to evil and be on the offensive against the hosts of darkness. The power and authority aren't intrinsic to the police person but rather derive from the laws and justice system the person's uniform and badge represent. He or she has been delegated to enforce this power and authority by the city/state/national government. Likewise, we have power and authority over demons, sickness, and even death because Jesus returned that authority to us through His crucifixion and resurrection. We represent Him on earth.

> Then Jesus came to them and said, "All authority in heaven and on earth has been given to me. Therefore go and make disciples of all nations, baptizing them in the name of the Father and of the Son and of the Holy Spirit."
> —Matthew 28:18–19

Even though we have great authority through Jesus, we must use this authority with humility and love. Jesus warns us that if someone sues us, we are to give him or her what he or she wants and more (Matthew 5:40). If the person hits us, we should turn the other cheek and not hit back (Matthew 5:39); we are to love and pray for our enemies (Matthew 5:44). Too often Christians use their authority without sensitivity.

> But in your hearts set apart Christ as Lord. Always be prepared to give an answer to everyone who asks you to give the reason for the hope that you have. But do this with gentleness and respect.
> —1 Peter 3:15

Spiritual Warfare

We must be sensitive to what the Holy Spirit wants us to do. We are told to love and bless and pray for our enemies (Luke 6:27–28). When we have intercessors praying and blessing people during our outreach events, the people we are trying to reach are very open. But if the intercessors pray to close down the psychics, the entire spiritual realm is stirred up, and people are agitated and usually won't talk with us. We do ask God to remove the stronghold of darkness, but we pray for and bless the people.

I was on an outreach in England, and I sensed the Holy Spirit warning me that I was about to encounter a psychic. Prior to such a power encounter, God will often let us know, so that we will have more boldness. I was walking up the street and noticed one of our dream teams in conversation with a woman, and there seemed to be some confusion. As I got closer, I realized the woman was naming close friends and family members of the team. Meanwhile, the team members were in awe of this woman's accuracy, but I discerned she was conjuring this information from a psychic spirit and not from God. As I stepped into the group, the Holy Spirit began to inform me about the woman. I gazed into her eyes and attested she was involved with something that was putting her child in danger. She stepped back a few feet, and her mouth hung open in surprise. When next she moved within a few inches of me and grabbed for my hands, I was able to recognize this as the encounter the Holy Spirit had foretold. Confident that God would accomplish something significant with this woman, I conceded to allow her to place her hands in mine, if she would afterward let me lay my hands on hers. She silently began to vibrate her thumb into my palms attempting to impart an evil spirit to me, yet as she did this, I calmly continued to stand there peering into her eyes, reminding her gently about God's power and His love for her. When she subsequently stopped, I took her hands and placed my thumbs in her palms (the way I often pray for people) and began to impart the Holy Spirit to her. At first she started to laugh hysterically; then the darkness in her eyes left. As God's presence came upon her, she began to sweat. By the time I gave her a revelatory word from God, that within eighteen months she would no longer be reading tarot cards but instead be serving Jesus, she broke loose from my grasp and ran off into the night.

I firmly believe God will honor that word over her, and she will come into relationship with Jesus Christ. I would never have done this unless God had counseled me to, and I don't recommend that you try it unless specifically directed by God, either. I am convinced God will cause our prophetic evangelism encounters to free her and others trapped in darkness, because ". . . the One who is in you is greater than the one who is in the world" (1 John 4:4).

On another occasion our teams had a booth and were offering dream interpretations at a large New Age event. Over the course of three days we interpreted more than two hundred dreams; in addition, four people allowed us to pray with them, during which time they were delivered from demonic forces right in the middle of the New Age event. Some were even so moved that they stayed at our booth for hours, just wanting to sit near us because they had never experienced such peace.

Often we will ask people: "Do you mind if we place our hands on you and ask the Creator to remove any obstacle to your coming into your full destiny? New light may come into your life as a result of this." When their hearts are compliant, people experience God's love and the Holy Spirit's presence. At times we've had more than thirty people at a time waiting for hours at our booth to receive this type of ministry.

All of our team members agree that these treasured episodes of bringing God's light into dark areas are the most fulfilling and enjoyable experiences they've had in their lives. God's desire is that we genuinely love people and exhibit His power to them—often without words. The more we become perfected in representing God faithfully in Spirit and truth—and not just mimicking a form of godliness that is inwardly weak and devoid of substance—the more we witness miracles; we see non-Christians desiring prayer and desperate to partake of the hope of glory we have in Christ (as well as the peace, contentment, joy, happiness, love, etc.).

Summary

Having read this book, I hope you will begin to consider new, creative ways of sharing God's love with people outside the Church. Millions of people today are starving for a profound encounter with God; they need real power to overcome their problems and nothing and no one else can assuage their thirst for the Spirit. Some visit churches in search of answers, yet leave before long unable to relate to Christians or connect with God. We are responsible to develop relationships with these seekers; we must disciple and walk with them through the rigorous process of growing in a relationship with Jesus Christ.

Many evangelistic methods Christians currently use in attempting to attract non-Christians are impersonal, outdated, and for several years have become generally ineffective on a large scale. Helping a person become a follower of Jesus requires more than a quick prayer on the street or receipt of a Bible pamphlet; it requires genuine prayer and care over time and awaiting divine openings for opportunities to impart more of God's truth to the person. Jesus loved people unconditionally; so must we.

When one traverses the crossroads of deciding to offer one's life to Jesus Christ, it is usually a result of a subliminal process involving time, circumstances, and events. Somehow, unfortunately, many of us have lost the sensitivity to discern who is ready to receive God's love. And while we would never consider forcing a rosebud open or expecting a newly planted seed to immediately become fully mature, we seem to lose sight of this principle in the life of a seeker. Assessing where a person is in his or her receptivity to committing to follow Jesus—come Heaven, hell, or high water—is one of the most important tools for successful evangelism.

Despite a cultural exposure in this country to what the Bible says, most of us underestimate and even sometimes negate the power of God's words. In addition, many professing Christians are unfamiliar with or have never either witnessed or experienced for themselves the Holy Spirit's power and presence.

A Message of Love

Demonstrating God's love is the most effective way to influence people for Jesus Christ. To accomplish this, we must believe God still speaks to us, that He still heals the sick, and that miracles still happen today. The God who performed the amazing exploits recorded in the Bible is *still* the same God today. He is still powerful and capable and willing. And He has given you and me the ability to hear His voice and to receive His unconditional love, through which we may then "feed [His] sheep . . . [and lambs]."

The word *gospel* means "good news." Spiritual seekers are scrutinizing our lives for indications that the "good news" has changed us. In order for them to be enticed, the good news has to be exponentially good! So, before we attempt to mess with anyone else, let's undergo the acid test to be sure God has truly and thoroughly transformed our lives from the inside out—that we consistently express Jesus' love and compassion no matter how we are received.

The fruit of the Spirit is love, joy, peace, patience, kindness, goodness, faithfulness, gentleness, and self-control (Galatians 5:22–23). These characteristics are the only invitations we can offer to entice non-Christians to really want to find and embrace a godly life. When you and I are wholeheartedly living for God, changed by His love, and oozing the Holy Spirit's nature (not just being good), then the world will want what we have, and we shall infect everyone we come in contact with—with divine truth in love.

Communicating with people outside the Church isn't an option but a necessity; however, we must meet them where they live. For even if they know about God, they often do not understand the "Christianese" we speak to describe Him.

The best way to be missionaries of God's love is to be ourselves.

People have radar to know when we are insincere; they will be drawn to us if we are genuine.

Speaking the Mysteries of God

Finally, as we engage more and more in "close encounters of the God kind," we will be called upon to use our spiritual gifts, to tear down walls of defensiveness. Then "God [will] open to us a door for the word, to speak the mystery of Christ, for which [we are] also in chains, that [we] may make it manifest . . ." (Colossians 4:3–4, NKJV). And they will share more unguardedly and honestly about the deeper issues in their lives.

After receiving a revelatory word from God or having a dream interpreted, people tend to be particularly open to talking about God. Let us, then, wield our God-given spiritual gifts as keys to unlock the door to people's hearts, open their spiritual eyes, and turn them from darkness to light (Acts 26:18).

Although my passion is to reach those involved in the New Age, I hope you can see that using process evangelism, spiritual gifts, and nonreligious language is a relevany means of reaching people in all walks of life.

My desire is not particularly that you go stand on a street corner with a sign heralding FREE SPIRITUAL READINGS; rather, I would have you be able to share with people how God sees them, in a way they are able to hear and understand at the same time, and thus bring lasting change to their lives.

NOTES

Chapter 1

1. The Streams Institute for Spiritual Development offers courses on *The Art of Hearing God, Understanding Dreams and Visions, Advanced Workshop in Dream Interpretation, Advanced Prophetic Ministry,* and *Reaching Your Destiny in God.* The courses are generally taught in an intensive two-and-a-half day format. For more information, see www.streamsministries.com.

Chapter 2

1. Tom Clegg and Warren Bird, *Lost in America* (Loveland, CO: Group Publishing, 2001), pp. 27–28.

2. George Barna, "Evangelism: Probability of Accepting Christ, Segmented by Age" (Barna Online Research, www.barna.org).

3. George Barna, "The Barna Update 2003: Spiritual Progress Hard to Find in 2003" (Barna Online Research, www.barna.org).

4. George Barna, "Barna Identifies Seven Paradoxes Regarding America's Faith" (Barna Online Research, www.barna.org, December 2002).

5. Steve Sjogren and Dave Ping, *Irresistible Evangelism: Natural Ways to Open Others Up to Jesus* (Loveland, CO: Group Publishing, 2004).

6. Lee Strobel, *Inside the Mind of Unchurched Harry and Mary* (Grand Rapids, MI: Zondervan Publishing, 1993).

7. Jesus' parables: Matthew 13:24–30; Matthew 13:33, Matthew 13:44; Matthew 22:2–14.

8. *Listening for Heaven's Sake: Building Genuine Trust and Openness* (Cincinnati, OH: Equipping Ministries International, www.equipmin.org).

Chapter 3

1. George Barna, "Born Again Adults Less Likely to Co-Habit, Just as Likely to Divorce" (Barna Online Research, www.barna.org, August 6, 2001).

2. George Barna, "Survey Shows Faith Impacts Some Behaviors But Not Others" (Barna Online Research, www.barna.org, October 2002).

3. Ed Matthews, "Mass Evangelism: Problems and Potentials," *Journal of Applied Missiology* 4 (1993).

4. The Alpha Course, www.alphacourse.org.

5. Kim Tau, Lost Heritage: *The Heroic Story of Radical Christianity* (Godalming, England: Highland Books, 1996) p. 195.

Chapter 4

1. Bill Hybels and Mark Mittelberg, *Becoming a Contagious Christian* (Grand Rapids, MI: Zondervan Publishing House, 1994), p. 155–162. Romans Road uses Romans 3:10, 23; 5:8–9; 6:23 to illustrate the Gospel message. The Bridge is a written illustration of how God and humanity separated when sin came into the world and how Jesus became the bridge back to God.

2. Evangelism Explosion International, P.O. Box 23820, Fort Lauderdale, FL 33307 (954) 491-6100, www.eeinternational.org.

3. Kim A. Lawton, "Evangelism Explosion Retools Its Approach," *Christianity Today*, vol. 41 (March 3, 1997), p. 58.

4. Michael Bolduc, *Power of Motivation* (Vancouver, BC: Guaranteed Success Strategies, www.guaranteedsuccess.com, 2002), pp. 42–43.

5. Don Richardson, *Eternity in Their Hearts* (Ventura, CA: Regal Books, 1984), pp. 130–131.

6. Ibid., back cover.

7. Ibid., p. 20.

8. The Shéma Yisrael Torah Network: Before life on earth begins, a person exists in his or her mother's womb and it is the source of sustenance. At birth, a person leaves the womb of his or her mother and enters the womb of earth. Earth is like the mother's womb because during a person's lifetime, it is the source of sustenance. Similarly, at death, a person leaves the womb of earth and enters the womb of creation. http://www.shemayisrael.co.il/burial/bur1.htm

Chapter 5

1. Steve Sjogren, *Conspiracy of Silence* (Ann Arbor, MI: Servant Publications, 1993), p. 63.

2. James Engel and Wilbert Norton, *What's Gone Wrong with the Harvest* (Grand Rapids, MI: Zondervan, 1975), p. 45.

3. John Wimber, *Power Evangelism: Equipping the Saints* (Anaheim, CA: Doin' the Stuff, 1985), p. 76.

4. George Barna, *Evangelism That Works: How to Reach Changing Generations with the Unchanging Gospel* (Ventura, CA: Regal Books, 1995), p. 41.

Chapter 6

1. Mark Stibbe, *Prophetic Evangelism: When God Speaks to Those Who Don't Know Him* (Milton Keynes, UK: Authentic Media, 2004), pp. xii-xiii. Used with permission.

Chapter 8

1. John Paul Jackson, "The Difference Between a Psychic and a Prophet," Catch the Fire Conference, St. Luke's Episcopal Church, Akron, OH, October 22, 1999.

2. John Paul Jackson, *"Prophets and Psychics," Course 101: The Art of Hearing God,* Streams Institute for Spiritual Development.

Chapter 9

1. Andy Butcher, "Christians Reach Olympic Crowds with Spiritual Readings," *Charisma,* April 2002, pp. 27–28, 30.

Chapter 10

1. Todd Bentley, "A New Kind of Power Evangelism Being Released—Over 460 Souls Saved in South Korea," article posted August 30, 2002 on www.revivalnow.com. Used with permission.

Chapter 11

1. John Paul Jackson, Streams Partner Letter, Streams Ministries International, August 2003. Used with permission.

ABOUT
the AUTHOR

I n 1985 Doug Addison had a dramatic encounter with Jesus just after having a reading done at the Berkley Institute for Psychics. Since that time, Doug's passion is to reach people who don't know God's love.

Doug has served as a pastor and church planter and was the National Dream Team Coordinator with John Paul Jackson's Streams Ministries. Currently Doug and his wife, Linda, reside in Los Angeles. Together they founded InLight Connection to help people come to know and understand God's love, acceptance, and power in their lives.

Doug teaches courses on hearing God, dreams and visions, and the supernatural. He also trains and leads dream team and prophetic and power evangelism outreaches throughout the United States and around the world.

For more information, please see **www.dougaddison.com**.

NO MORE CHRISTIANESE
by Doug Addison

Give people words of encouragement in simple, everyday language. This glossary and teaching guide will help you communicate God's heart for others without sounding religious.

Paperback
Price: $5

NO MORE CHRISTIANESE CD

An indepth teaching on why and how to communicate with others without sounding religious. A perfect companion to the booklet.

1-CD Set
Price: $7

DREAM SECRETS
by Doug Addison

Discover the hidden meaning of your dreams. This informative and funny audio message will help you to find the meaning to many common dreams.

1-CD Set
Price: $7

4 KEYS TO
RELEVANT EVANGELISM
by Doug Addison

In this CD, Doug Addison reveals how we can demonstrate God's love and power to people that leaves them wanting to hear more. You'll learn how to interact with people and the power of encouraging words.

1-CD Set
Price: $7

MOMENTS WITH GOD
DREAM JOURNAL
by John Paul Jackson

John Paul Jackson shares his unique approach to dream recording
and offers important keys to unearthing rewarding spiritual
insights into your dreams. Included in this journal are three color
wheels, sample journal entries, and specially designed forms to
record your dreams and begin a dream dictionary.

Hardback
Price: $24

UNDERSTANDING DREAMS AND VISIONS
by John Paul Jackson

Explore the world of dreams. Unravel the mysteries of dream interpretation in this inspiring series. Discover how to apply God-given insights in your waking life.

6-CD Set
Price: $42

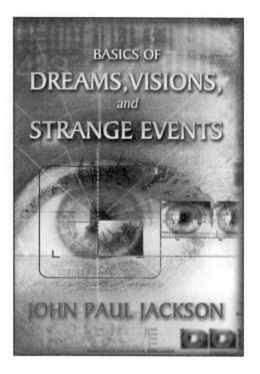

BASICS OF DREAMS, VISIONS, AND STRANGE EVENTS
by John Paul Jackson

A pioneer of biblical dream interpretation, John Paul Jackson guides you through the supernatural realm that interacts and coexists with us. You'll discover patterns and rhythms of God's nighttime metaphors.

2-CD Set
Price: $17

STREAMS INSTITUTE FOR SPIRITUAL DEVELOPMENT

John Paul Jackson, Founder

At Streams, we seek to give shape to ideas that educate, inform, and cause people to better understand and delight in God. We endeavor to enrich people's lives by satisfying their lifelong need to identify and use their God-given gifts. We seek to be used by God to heal, renew, and encourage pastors and church leaders.

Courses offered include:

Course 101: The Art of Hearing God
Course 102: Advanced Prophetic Ministry
Course 104: Reaching Your Destiny in God
Course 201: Understanding Dreams and Visions
Course 202: Advanced Workshop in Dream Interpretation

More information is available online at
www.streamsministries.com or by calling **1.888.441.8080**